Copyright 1997

by

Jian Fan

ACKNOWLEDGEMENTS

First, I would like to express my deep gratitude to my advisor, Andrew Laine, for all his support and encouragement. I thank him for introducing me to the field of wavelets, and I appreciate the opportunity to work with him.

I would like to thank Dr. Jerry C. L. Chen and Mrs. Shirley H. W. Chen of Palo Alto, California, for their help and support. Without their support, I may not have the opportunity to pursue my graduate studies in the United States.

I would like to thank Drs. Gerhard Ritter, Sartaj Sahni, Dave Wilson and John G. Harris for being on my thesis committee, and Dr. Baba C. Vemuri for attending my defense. Their time and thoughtful recommendations were greatly appreciated.

I would also like to thank Dr. David Burchfield of the Department of Pediatrics, University of Florida, for providing me a graduate research assistantship from January 1991 through December 1991.

During my early years at the University of Florida, Ming Jiang and Min Shi gave me much help. I also benefited greatly from discussions with my follow graduate students, Shuwu Song, Iztok Koren, Sergio Schuler, Wuhai Yang, Chun-ming Chang and Hongchi Shi.

In addition, I would like to thank my manager Catherine Hunt of Hewlett Packard Company, San Diego, for her support. I have also benefited from Hewlett-Packard Company's educational assistance program. I appreciate the efforts of John Shumate who helped polish the writing of this dissertation.

Finally, I would like to thank my mother Yuzhen Chen and my late father Laikun Fan for their inspiration and encouragement, as well as my wife Weihua Liu and my son Xiying Fan for their understanding, love, and patience.

This research was supported in part by the Whitaker Foundation, and the U. S. Army Medical Research and Development Command, Grand number DAMD17-93-J-3003.

TABLE OF CONTENTS

ACKNOWLEDGEMENTS iii

LIST OF TABLES viii

LIST OF FIGURES ix

ABSTRACT xi

CHAPTERS

1 INTRODUCTION 1

   1.1 Motivations of the Research 1
   1.2 Review of Related Work 2
   1.3 Overview of the Thesis 4

2 SIGNAL REPRESENTATIONS AND CONVOLUTION OPERATORS 5

   2.1 Introduction 5
   2.2 Fourier Transforms 6
      2.2.1 Fourier Transform (FT) 7
      2.2.2 Discrete-time Fourier Transform (DTFT) 7
      2.2.3 Short-time Fourier Transform (STFT) 8
      2.2.4 Discrete-time Short-time Fourier Transform (DTSTFT) . 8
      2.2.5 Connection Between Short-time Fourier Transform and
           Filter Banks 9
      2.2.6 Generalized Short-time Fourier Transform 10
   2.3 Wavelet Transforms 10
      2.3.1 Continuous Wavelet Transform (CWT) 11
      2.3.2 Discrete Wavelet Transform (DWT) 12
      2.3.3 Discrete-time Wavelet Transform (DTWT) 13
   2.4 Generalized Discrete-time Filter Bank Transforms 15
      2.4.1 Convolution Operator on Complete Representations . . . 17
      2.4.2 Convolution Operator on Overcomplete Representations 19
      2.4.3 Approximation of Convolution Operators on Overcomplete
           Representations 19
      2.4.4 Aliasing Enhancement on Complete Representations . . . 20
   2.5 Summary and Discussion 22

3 OVERCOMPLETE WAVELET REPRESENTATIONS 23

   3.1 Introduction 23
   3.2 Overcomplete Wavelet Transforms and Filters 23
       3.2.1 Overcomplete Wavelet Packet Representations 23
       3.2.2 Dyadic Wavelet Representations 25
       3.2.3 Filters of Autocorrelation Functions of Wavelets 28
   3.3 Connection to Complete Wavelet Representations 29
   3.4 Time-frequency Interpretation and the Uncertainty Principle . . 29
   3.5 Two-dimensional Extensions 34

4 OPERATIONS ON OVERCOMPLETE WAVELET REPRESENTATIONS 37

   4.1 Introduction 37
   4.2 Gain Operators 37
       4.2.1 Minimum Mean Square Error (MMSE) Approximation . . 38
       4.2.2 Time-frequency Trade-off and a Greedy Algorithm 40
   4.3 Shrinking Operators 42
   4.4 Envelope Detectors 44
       4.4.1 Envelope Detection by Hilbert Transform 47
       4.4.2 Envelope Detection by Zero Crossings 49
       4.4.3 Comparison Between the Two Detectors 50
       4.4.4 Comparison with Other Energy Operators 50
       4.4.5 Two Dimensional Envelope Detection 50

5 APPLICATION I: TEXTURE SEGMENTATION 53

   5.1 Introduction 53
   5.2 Texture Feature Extraction 54
   5.3 Considerations on Filter Selection 55
   5.4 The Basic Isodata Clustering Algorithm 57
   5.5 Postprocessing 58
   5.6 Experimental Results 58
       5.6.1 One-dimensional Signals 58
       5.6.2 Natural Textures 59
       5.6.3 Synthetic Textures 62
   5.7 Summary and Discussion 62

6 APPLICATION II: IMAGE DEBLURRING 66

   6.1 Introduction 66
   6.2 Review of Some Deblurring Techniques 67
       6.2.1 Modified Inverse Filters 67
       6.2.2 Wiener Filters 68
       6.2.3 Wavelet-Vaguelette Inversion 69
       6.2.4 Discussion 70
   6.3 Discrete-time Overcomplete Wavelet Packet Inversion 72
       6.3.1 One-dimensional Formulation 72
       6.3.2 Two-dimensional Extension 74
   6.4 Experimental Results 75
       6.4.1 One-dimensional Signals 78
       6.4.2 Two-dimensional Images 81
   6.5 Summary and Discussion 82

7   CONCLUSION   86

APPENDIXES

   A   PROOFS RELATED TO DISCRETE-TIME WAVELETS   88

   B   NUMERICAL COMPUTATION OF BATTLE-LEMARIÉ WAVELET   95

      B.1   Functions in Finite Terms   95
      B.2   Numerical Computation Using FFT   99

   C   NUMERICAL COMPUTATION OF THE UNCERTAINTY FACTOR   103

   D   BOUNDARY TREATMENTS OF FINITE-LENGTH SEQUENCES .   107

      D.1   Periodic Extensions   107
      D.2   Closure of Symmetry Under Convolution   107

REFERENCES   111

BIOGRAPHICAL SKETCH   115

LIST OF TABLES

3.1 Uncertainty Factors of Analyzing Filters 34

5.1 Boundary Accuracy of the Segmentation Results. 64

6.1 Performance of 1D Deblurring Examples 81

6.2 Performance of 2D Deblurring Examples 82

B.1 Coefficients of $g_{24}(x)$ (a) and Truncated Impulse Response of $h_1(n)$ (b). 100

LIST OF FIGURES

2.1 A Filter Bank Implementation of STFT. 10

2.2 Fast Discrete-time Wavelet Transform–First Two Levels. 13

2.3 Generalized Discrete-time Filter Bank Transform. 15

2.4 Example of General Binary-tree-structured Filter Bank of Five Channels. 16

2.5 The Overcomplete Wavelet Transform for the Example of Figure 2.4. 17

2.6 Example of the Aliasing-enhancement Anomaly. 21

3.1 Binary Tree for Overcomplete Wavelet Packet Decomposition 24

3.2 Binary Tree for Dyadic Wavelet Decomposition. 26

3.3 Examples of the Function $\Theta_{a,b}(\omega)$. 27

3.4 Two Examples of the Overcomplete Wavelet Representation. 30

3.5 Examples of Time-frequency Localization by Overcomplete Wavelet
    Packet Representations. 32

3.6 Uncertainty factors (drawn on top of each band) of Channel Filters. . 33

4.1 Examples of Gain Vector Approximation 41

4.2 Examples of the Minimum Tree Approximation with the Maximum
    Depth of Seven Levels. 43

4.3 An Example of Overcomplete Wavelet Denoising. 45

4.4 Comparison of Overcomplete Wavelet Shrinkage Denoising with Linear
    Smoothing Using the Signal of (row 1,col 1) of Figure 4.3. 46

4.5 Two Examples of Power Density Distribution of Overcomplete Wavelet
    Packet Representations. 48

4.6 A FIR Hilbert Transformer 49

4.7 Comparison of the Two Envelope Detectors. 51

4.8 Frequency Response of Equivalent Complex Quadrature Filters (level 1). 52

5.1   Segmentation of a 1D Signal Consists of Triangular Waveform and
        Sinusoid.   59

5.2   Segmentation of a Noisy 1D Signal Consists of Two Pure Tone Segments   60

5.3   Segmentation Results of a Image Consist of Natural Textures.   61

5.4   Segmentation of a Synthetic Gaussian Lowpassed Texture Image . . .   63

5.5   Segmentation of a Synthetic FIN Texture Image   63

5.6   Segmentation of a Synthetic Texture Image with Line Patterns. . . .   64

6.1   Log Frequency Responses of Filters for a Gaussian Blur   76

6.2   Log Frequency Responses of Filters for an uniform Blur   77

6.3   One-dimensional Deblurrings of a Gaussian Blur.   79

6.4   One-dimensional Deblurrings of an Uniform Blur.   80

6.5   Deblurring a Gaussian-blurred Lena Image.   83

6.6   Deblurring an Uniform-blurred Lena Image.   84

A.1   Equivalent Structures for (a) Convolution and Decimation and
        (b) Expansion and Convolution.   91

A.2   Illustration of Adding One More Channel by Splitting a Channel into
        Two.   92

B.1   Transition Band of Filters $H_p(\omega)$ with $p = 1, 3, 9$.   101

C.1   Channel Bandwidths of Overcomplete Wavelet Representations. . . .   104

Abstract of Dissertation Presented to the Graduate School
of the University of Florida in Partial Fulfillment of the
Requirements for the Degree of Doctor of Philosophy

OVERCOMPLETE WAVELET REPRESENTATIONS
WITH APPLICATIONS IN IMAGE PROCESSING

By

Jian Fan

August 1997

Chairman: Dr. Andrew F. Laine
Major Department: Computer and Information Science and Engineering

Orthogonal wavelet transforms have been applied to the field of signal and
image processing with promising results in compression and denoising. Coefficients of
such a transform constitute a complete representation of a signal without redundancy.
However, there are applications where complete representations are disadvantageous.
In this thesis, we examine classes of Fourier transforms and wavelet transforms in
terms of their efficacy of representing convolution operators. We have identified two
shortcomings associated with complete representations of the discrete-time domain:
(1) the lack of translation invariance and the (2) a possible anomaly of aliasing-
enhancement.

On the other hand, our analysis showed that overcomplete wavelet representations do not bear those shortcomings of their non-redundant counterparts. Our
framework of overcomplete wavelet representations include construction algorithms

and prototype filters, spatial-frequency interpretation and three operations. Capabilities of spatial-frequency localization were quantitatively evaluated using uncertainty factors. Associated with gain, shrinking and envelope operators, algorithms for convolution, denoising and analysis of power density distribution were presented and analyzed.

The framework of overcomplete wavelet representations was then applied to segmentation of textured images and image deblurring. We demonstrated that envelopes as feature vectors performed well in segmenting both natural and synthetic textures. We showed that gain and shrinking operators may be used for image deblurring and discuss limitations of the methodology.

CHAPTER 1
INTRODUCTION

1.1 Motivations of the Research

In the past decade, wavelets have stimulated great interests in many fields of applied mathematics and engineering, generating a significant amount of research activities. Within these fields, traditional theories and techniques have been reevaluated to explore opportunities for wavelet applications.

Although continuous time wavelets possess mathematical elegance, discrete-time wavelet transforms are of special importance for practical applications. Among them, discrete-time orthogonal wavelet transforms have gained popularity. Coefficients of such a transform constitute a complete representation of a signal without redundancy. Complete representations have produced promising results in image compression and denoising. However, there are applications where complete representations are disadvantageous. Understanding the strength and weakness of various representations and the relationships among them is essential for satisfying intellectual inquires and developing new methodologies. In this thesis, we considered both classes of Fourier-based representations and wavelet-based representations with emphasis in the discrete-time domain. We found that the overcomplete wavelet representations served to bridge the two classes.

The merit of a particular representation should be judged by its capability to facilitate solving problems. Two important but difficult problems, segmentation of textured images and image deblurring, were selected as benchmarks. Accordingly, we value a representation by its capability to extract certain features from signals, efficacy of representing an operation and invariance under certain operations.

With the understanding of various representations and the problems in hand, we developed a framework of discrete-time overcomplete wavelet representation. The framework included construction algorithms and prototype filters, time-frequency interpretation and three operations. Algorithms associated with gain operators, shrinking operators and envelope detectors were developed. The framework of overcomplete wavelet representations was then applied to segmentation of textured images and image deblurring. This demonstrated that envelopes as feature vectors performed well in segmenting both natural and synthetic textures. For the deblurring application, our formulation extended the wavelet-vaguelette inversion into discrete-time domain and was applicable to more blurring sources.

1.2 Review of Related Work

On the general topic of wavelet theory, a brief history and comprehensive review were included in Jawerth and Sweldens' survey [32]. The papers by Daubechies [11] and Mallat [42, 41] were considered influential for the recent developments. The paper by another wavelet pioneer Strang [59] was also explanatory. The orthonormal wave packet bases is a generalization of orthogonal wavelets, was introduced by Coifman and Meyer [10]. The book by Daubechies [13] included in-depth mathematical discussions and real design examples. The book by Vaidyanathan [63], which was written for signal processing audience, provided much insight into the relationship between wavelets and multirate filter banks.

The lack of translation invariance of discrete-time orthogonal wavelets was recognized as a major shortcoming for pattern recognition by many researchers [41, 59]. Various proposals were made to address the issue. Multiscale edge representations were investigated by Mallat and Zhong [44], Mallat and Hwang [43], and Berman and Baras [5]. Steerable filters with shiftabilities were studied by Simoncelli *et al.* [58]. A orthogonal representation with invariance of the subband structure was proposed by Pesquet *et al.* [52].

Using energy distribution in subbands of wavelet packet decomposition as signatures for texture classification was presented by Laine and Fan [36]. A similar approach was also reported by Chang and Kuo [8]. Earlier results using envelopes of overcomplete wavelet packet representation for texture segmentation was reported by Laine and Fan [35]. A simplified version of Chapter 5 of this thesis was later published [37]. The overcomplete wavelet representation was also used by User [62] with an ad hoc feature extraction algorithm. A methodology combining Markov random field and orthogonal wavelet packet transform was described by Bello [4].

The nonlinear wavelet shrinkage for denoising was due to Donoho and Johnstone [17]. The approach was applied to power spectrum estimation [48], and to medical image processing [1]. Nonlinear denoising based on wavelet maxima representation by Mallat and Hwang shared some similar ideas [43], although tracing singularities through the scale space turned out to be much more difficult, especially in a two-dimensional space.

Manipulating wavelet representations to enhance certain features is obviously a good idea. Jawerth *et al.* [31] reported image enhancement using weight factors to modify coefficients of orthogonal wavelet transforms. Laine *et al.* [38] demonstrated various approaches for enhancement of digital mammographic images. Fan and Laine [20] pointed out the connection between linear gain enhancement using overcomplete dyadic wavelet representations and the unsharp masking, and introduced a nonlinear function for contrast enhancement. However, due to the lack of an objective definition of image quality, those enhancement algorithms were mostly ad hoc and hard to evaluate. On the other hand, image deblurring is considered to be a well defined problem. The approach adapted by Banham *et al.* [3] is to decompose the linear minimum mean square error (LMMSE) filters into the orthogonal transform domain with advantage of reduced alliance on the assumption of global stationarity. However, their proposal was basically the linear filtering and no optimal subband selection was considered. The mathematical framework of the wavelet-vaguelette inversion was due to Donoho [14, 16]. The limitations were that it was derived on the continuous time domain and inapplicable to some common sources such as Gaussian and uniform blurs.

1.3 Overview of the Thesis

This thesis is organized as follows:

Chapter 2 reviews signal representations derived from the Fourier transform and the wavelet transform in the context of being operated upon by a convolution operator. The scrutiny reveals that complete representations suffer from not being translation invariant and the existence of the aliasing-enhancement anomaly, and are thus inappropriate for certain applications.

Chapter 3 presents the framework of the overcomplete wavelet representation with two particular building algorithm and filters. The time-frequency localization property of overcomplete wavelet representations is examined under the uncertainty principle.

Chapter 4 introduces gain, shrinking and envelope operators applicable upon an overcomplete wavelet representation. Algorithms for determining specific parameters are detailed with examples and comparisons shown. Both Chapter 5 and 6 are applications of the theory of overcomplete wavelet representations developed in previous chapters.

Chapter 5 deals with the topic of image texture segmentation. The segmentation problem is formulated in the paradigm of spatial-frequency analysis, and a texture feature based on the concept of power density distribution is proposed.

Chapter 6 addresses the problem of image deblurring using the gain operator for deconvolution and the shrinking operator for nonlinear denoising.

Chapter 7 concludes the research and proposes future directions.

CHAPTER 2
SIGNAL REPRESENTATIONS AND CONVOLUTION OPERATORS

2.1 Introduction

For a given signal x, it is often beneficial to transform (map) x into another form (domain), denoted $x \overset{M}{\mapsto} X$. X is called the representation of x in the transform domain. Instead of directly dealing with the original signal x, we may deal with its representation X. By doing so we usually transform a particular problem into a different form and make it easier to solve. Clearly, different applications demand different representations.

The applications considered in this thesis are texture image segmentation and image deblurring. Accordingly, the time-invariability and the efficacy of representations are the most important factors. Both properties may be revealed by their behavior under a convolution operator. With these in mind, we shall review Fourier transforms and wavelet transforms of one dimensional signals. To facilitate our discussions, we used the following basic definitions:

Definition 2.1.1 (Translation Operator) *For a continuous function $x(t)$, a translation operator is defined as $T_s[x(t)] = x(t-s)$; For a discrete function $x(n)$, a translation operator is defined as $T_d[x(n)] = x(n-d)$.*

Definition 2.1.2 (Convolution Operator) *For a continuous function $f(t)$, a convolution operator is defined as $T_f[x(t)] = x(t) * f(t) = \int_{-\infty}^{\infty} x(\tau)f(t-\tau)d\tau$; For a discrete function $x(n)$, a convolution operator is defined as $T_f[x(n)] = x(n) * f(n) = \sum_{m=-\infty}^{+\infty} x(m)f(n-m)$. The functions $f(t)$ and $f(n)$ are called the kernel. Notice that a translation operator is a special convolution operator with kernel $f(t) = \delta(t-\tau)$*

$(f(n) = \delta(n - d))$. *Therefore, we will use T for both translation and convolution operators.*

Definition 2.1.3 (Eigenfunction and Eigenvalue) *For a linear operator T, if there exists a function e, such that $T[e] = \lambda e$, where λ is a constant, the function e is called the eigenfunction of T, and the value λ is called the eigenvalue.*

Definition 2.1.4 (Translation invariant) *For a given signal x, a translation operator T and a mapping operator $\mathcal{M}$, if the two operators are commutable such that*

$$\mathcal{M}[T(x)] = T[\mathcal{M}(x)],$$

the mapping is called translation invariant, and the representation X is said to be a translation invariant representation.

2.2 Fourier Transforms

Frequency-domain representation by Fourier transform played a major role in signal analysis and linear system theory [51, 49, 63]. The efficacy of Fourier representation is due to the fact that its basis functions of complex exponentials are eigenfunctions of a convolution operator [49, page 39]. For a linear convolution operator T, the eigenequation is:

$$T_f\left[e^{j\omega t}\right] = F(\omega)e^{j\omega t},$$

where eigenvalue $F(\omega)$ is the Fourier transform of $f(t)$. An almost identical form can be derived for the discrete-time Fourier transform. Fourier representations are particularly powerful for signal deblurring since it transforms a deconvoltuion problem into the simple form of divisions.

However, Fourier representations may not be good at capturing frequency evolution over time. As time variable is added to Fourier transforms, basis functions of short-time Fourier transforms are no longer eigenfunctions of a convolution operator.

2.2.1 Fourier Transform (FT)

The Fourier transform pair may be written as:

$$X(\omega) = \int_{-\infty}^{\infty} x(t)e^{-j\omega t}dt \qquad (FT),$$
$$x(t) = \frac{1}{2\pi}\int_{-\infty}^{\infty} X(\omega)e^{j\omega t}d\omega \quad (Inverse\ FT).$$

A linear convolution operator T_f can be characterized by

$$y(t) = T_f\left[x(t)\right] = \int_{-\infty}^{\infty} X(\omega)T_f\left[e^{j\omega t}\right]d\omega = \int_{-\infty}^{\infty} X(\omega)F(\omega)e^{j\omega t}d\omega,$$

or,

$$Y(\omega) = X(\omega)F(\omega).$$

This shows that Fourier representation of the convolution operator T is the Fourier transform of its kernel. The beauty of this representation is that on the Fourier domain, a convolution (deconvolution) is simply multiplications (divisions) of the both representations.

For a translation operator with kernel $f(t) = \delta(t-s)$, $F(\omega) = e^{-j\omega s}$, and therefore $|Y(\omega)| = |X(\omega)|$, which means that *magnitude* of Fourier transform is *translation invariant*.

2.2.2 Discrete-time Fourier Transform (DTFT)

The discrete-time Fourier transform may be written as [49]:

$$X(e^{j\omega}) = \sum_{n=-\infty}^{\infty} x(n)e^{-j\omega n} \qquad (DTFT),$$
$$x(n) = \frac{1}{2\pi}\int_{-\pi}^{\pi} X(e^{j\omega})e^{j\omega n}d\omega \quad (Inverse\ DTFT).$$

Similar to its continuous counterpart,

$$y(n) = T_f\left[x(n)\right] = \frac{1}{2\pi}\int_{-\pi}^{\pi} X(e^{j\omega})F(e^{j\omega})e^{j\omega n}d\omega,$$

or,

$$Y(e^{j\omega}) = X(e^{j\omega})F(e^{j\omega}).$$

For a translation operator with $f(n) = \delta(n - d)$, $F(e^{j\omega}) = e^{-j\omega d}$ and thus $|Y(e^{j\omega})| = |X(e^{j\omega})|$.

2.2.3 Short-time Fourier Transform (STFT)

In order to capture frequency evolution of a non-stationary signal, a window $w(t)$ is introduced into the Fourier transform. The short-time Fourier transform may be written as:

$$X(\omega, t) = \int_{-\infty}^{\infty} x(\tau)w(t - \tau)e^{-j\omega\tau}d\tau \quad (STFT),$$

$$x(t) = \frac{1}{2\pi w(0)} \int_{-\infty}^{\infty} X(\omega, t)e^{j\omega t}d\omega \quad (Inverse \; STFT).$$

where we assumed $w(0) \neq 0$.

For a convolution operator T_f,

$$T_f \left[w(t - \tau)e^{j\omega t} \right] = F(\omega, t - \tau)e^{j\omega t},$$

where $F(\omega, t)$ is the STFT representation of the kernel $f(t)$. It means that in general the windowed complex exponentials are no longer eigenfunctions of a convolution operator. Consequently, STFT representation of $y(t) = T_f[x(t)]$ is another convolution of either

$$Y(\omega, t) = \int_{-\infty}^{\infty} F(\omega, t - \tau)x(\tau)e^{-j\omega\tau}d\tau,$$

or,

$$Y(\omega, t) = \int_{-\infty}^{\infty} X(\omega, t - \tau)f(\tau)e^{-j\omega\tau}d\tau.$$

For a translation operator with $f(t) = \delta(t - s)$, $Y(\omega, t) = X(\omega, t - s)e^{-j\omega s}$, and thus $|Y(\omega, t)| = |X(\omega, t - s)|$. Therefore, magnitude of STFT transform is a time-invariant representation.

2.2.4 Discrete-time Short-time Fourier Transform (DTSTFT)

The discrete-time short-time Fourier transform may be written as [49, 53]

$$X(e^{j\omega}, n) = \sum_{k=-\infty}^{\infty} x(k)w(n - k)e^{-j\omega k}, \quad (DTSTFT) \tag{2.1}$$

$$x(n) = \frac{1}{2\pi w(0)} \int_{-\pi}^{\pi} X(e^{j\omega}, n)e^{j\omega n}d\omega. \; (Inverse \; DTSTFT) \tag{2.2}$$

For a discrete convolution operator T_f and $y(n) = T_f[x(n)]$, we have

$$Y(e^{j\omega}, n) = \sum_{k=-\infty}^{\infty} X(e^{j\omega}, n - k)f(k)e^{-j\omega k},$$

or,

$$Y(e^{j\omega}, n) = \sum_{k=-\infty}^{\infty} F(e^{j\omega}, n - k)x(k)e^{-j\omega k}.$$

For a translation operator T_f with $f(n) = \delta(n-k)$, $|Y(e^{j\omega}, n)| = |X(e^{j\omega}, n - k)|$. Thus, the magnitude of DTSTFT is also a *translation-invariant* representation.

2.2.5 Connection Between Short-time Fourier Transform and Filter Banks

The discrete-time short-time Fourier transform $X(e^{j\omega}, n)$ is a two-dimensional function of a continuous variable ω and a integer variable n. Is it possible to have only finite samples $X(e^{j\omega_k}, n)$ in the frequency domain, and yet still able to recover the original signal $x(n)$? It turns out to be possible by carefully designing channel filters [63, 53].

For a given frequency ω_k, STFT coefficients of (2.1) can be rewritten as

$$X(e^{j\omega_k}, n) = e^{-j\omega_k n} \sum_{m=-\infty}^{\infty} x(m)w(n - m)e^{j\omega_k(n-m)} = e^{-j\omega_k n}\left[x(n) * v_k(n)\right],$$

where $v_k(n) = w(n)e^{j\omega_k n}$. This means that a frequency point of STFT can be computed using a filter with frequency response $V_k(\omega) = W(\omega - \omega_k)$ and a complex multiplier $e^{-j\omega_k n}$. Note that $|X(e^{j\omega_k}, n)| = |x(n) * v_k(n)|$.

For a filter bank consists of $M - 1$ such channels satisfying

$$\sum_{k=0}^{M-1} V_k(\omega) = \sum_{k=0}^{M-1} W(\omega - \omega_k) = 1, \tag{2.3}$$

the original function $x(n)$ can be recovered by replacing the integral of (2.2) with the following summation:

$$\sum_{k=0}^{M-1} X(e^{j\omega_k}, n)e^{j\omega_k n} = \sum_{k=0}^{M-1}\left[x(n) * v_k(n)\right] = x(n) * \left[\sum_{k=0}^{M-1} v_k(n)\right] \overset{(2.3)}{=} x(n).$$

Figure 2.1 showed a filter bank structure for the analysis-synthesis process of STFT.

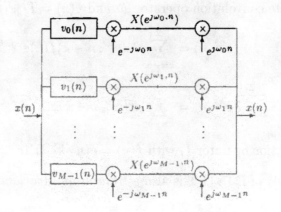

Figure 2.1: A Filter Bank Implementation of STFT.

2.2.6   Generalized Short-time Fourier Transform

We already pointed out that STFT magnitude can be computed by a filter bank without modulators and demodulators (see Figure 2.1). We can further relax the constraint that channel filters are frequency-shifted of a single lowpass filter $v(n)$, and define a generalized short-time Fourier transform pair as

$$w_k(n) = \sum_{m=-\infty}^{\infty} x(m)v_k(n-m), \ 0 \le k \le M - 1,$$

$$x(n) = \sum_{k=0}^{M-1} w_k(n) .$$

2.3   Wavelet Transforms

Wavelet transforms have become a powerful tool for analyzing non-stationary signals in recent years. It has several major advantages over the short-time Fourier transform.

First, wavelet transforms choose to fix the ratio of bandwidth/center-frequency (called *constant-Q*) of channel frequency response instead of the frequency resolution (determined by the bandwidth of the window) as in STFT. In other words, wavelet transforms use a narrow bandwidth window for low frequency signals and a wide bandwidth window for high frequency signals. The idea behind this is that low frequency components represent slow changes in the time domain for which time resolution is not critical while higher resolution in the frequency domain is more desirable. In the opposite case, a wide bandwidth window for high frequency components means better resolution in the time domain to capture abrupt changes.

Second, recent development of wavelet packet transforms and other signal-adaptive wavelet-type transforms are much more flexible and powerful in exploiting time-frequency concept for wide-ranging applications.

2.3.1 Continuous Wavelet Transform (CWT)

For a continuous time signal $x(t)$, a continuous wavelet transform pair may be written as [41, 12]:

$$X(a, \tau) = \int_{-\infty}^{\infty} x(u)\psi_a^*(u - \tau)du \qquad (CWT), \qquad (2.4)$$

$$x(t) = \frac{1}{C_\psi} \int_{\tau=-\infty}^{\tau=\infty} \int_{a=0}^{a=\infty} X(a, \tau)\psi_a(t - \tau)d\tau \frac{da}{a^2} \; (Inverse \; CWT). \qquad (2.5)$$

where x^* denotes complex conjugate of x, $\psi_a(t) = \frac{1}{\sqrt{a}}\psi(\frac{t}{a})$. $\psi(t)$ is called the basic wavelet. Parameter τ is the translation factor and a is the dilation factor. Informally speaking, when a increases, function $\psi_a(t - \tau)$ expands and takes long-time behavior into account. In the opposite, when a decreases, function $\psi_a(t - \tau)$ contracts and only focuses on the short-time behavior. In order to recover the original signal from its CWT, the wavelet $\psi(t)$ must satisfy the *admissibility condition*:

$$C_\psi = \int_0^\infty \frac{|\Psi(\omega)|^2}{\omega}d\omega < +\infty.$$

However, a wavelet function $\psi_a(t)$ is generally not an eigenfunction of a convolution operator T, as:

$$T_f[\psi_a(t)] = \int_{-\infty}^{\infty} f(\xi)\psi_a(t - \xi)d\xi$$

does not equal to $\lambda\psi_a(t)$.

Since inverse CWT of (2.5) can be rewritten as:

$$x(t) = \frac{1}{C_\psi} \int_{a=0}^{a=\infty} [X(a,t) * \psi_a(t)] \frac{da}{a^2} ,$$

where $*$ denotes convolution on variable t, we have:

$$T_f[x(t)] = \frac{1}{C_\psi} \int_0^\infty [(f(t) * X(a,t)) * \psi_a(t)] \frac{da}{a^2} .$$

If we denote $\mathcal{W}$ as the operator of continuous wavelet transform, the above result showed:

$$\mathcal{W}T_f[x(t)] = f(t) * X(a,t) = \int_{-\infty}^\infty f(\xi)X(a, \tau - \xi)d\xi = T_f\mathcal{W}[x(t)] .$$

Therefore, CWT is a translation invariant representation.

2.3.2 Discrete Wavelet Transform (DWT)

Discrete wavelet transform pair on real orthogonal wavelet bases may be written as [63]:

$$\mu_j(n) = \int_{-\infty}^\infty x(t)2^{-j/2}\psi(2^{-j}t - n)dt \quad (DWT),$$

$$x(t) = \sum_{j=0}^{+\infty} \sum_{n=-\infty}^{+\infty} \mu_j(n)2^{-j/2}\psi(2^{-j}t - n) \quad (Inverse\ DWT).$$

where functions $\left\{2^{-j/2}\psi(2^{-j}t - n)\right\}$ consist an orthonomal basis.

Notice that DWT maps a continuous-time function $x(t)$ into a discrete-time sequence $\mu_j(n)$. Clearly, it is not a translation invariant representation.

As in the case of CWT, basis functions $2^{-j/2}\psi(2^{-j}t - n)$ generally is not a eigenfunction of convolution operators. However, $T_f\left[2^{-j/2}\psi(2^{-j}t - n)\right]$ may be decomposed in DWT space:

$$T_f\left[2^{-j/2}\psi(2^{-j}t - n)\right] = \sum_{l=0}^{+\infty} \sum_{m=-\infty}^{+\infty} \nu_{j,l}(n,m)2^{-l/2}\psi(2^{-l}t - m),$$

where the transform coefficients may be calculated by:

$$\nu_{j,l}(n,m) = \int_{-\infty}^\infty T_f\left[2^{-j/2}\psi(2^{-j}t - n)\right] 2^{-l/2}\psi(2^{-l}t - m)dt$$

$$= \int_{-\infty}^\infty \left[\int_{-\infty}^\infty f(\xi)2^{-j/2}\psi\left(2^{-j}(t - \xi) - n\right) d\xi\right] 2^{-l/2}\psi(2^{-l}t - m)dt$$

$$= 2^{-(j+l)/2} \int_{-\infty}^\infty f(\xi) \left[\int_{-\infty}^\infty \psi\left(2^{-j}(t - \xi) - n\right) \psi(2^{-l}t - m)dt\right] d\xi.$$

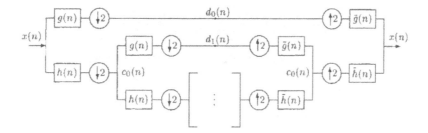

Figure 2.2: Fast Discrete-time Wavelet Transform–First Two Levels.
Note: Down arrow = decimation and up arrow = expansion.

We can derive DWT representation of $T_f[x(t)]$ to be

$$
\begin{aligned}
T_f[x(t)] &= \sum_{j=0}^{+\infty} \sum_{n=-\infty}^{+\infty} \mu_j(n) T_f\left[2^{-j/2}\psi(2^{-j}t - n)\right] \\
&= \sum_{l=0}^{+\infty} \sum_{m=-\infty}^{+\infty} \left[\sum_{j=0}^{+\infty} \sum_{n=-\infty}^{+\infty} \mu_j(n)\nu_{j,l}(n,m)\right] 2^{-l/2}\psi(2^{-l}t - m) .
\end{aligned}
$$

Therefore, $\{\nu_{j,l}(n,m)\}$ can be seen as representation of the operator T_f under the basis $\{2^{-j/2}\psi(2^{-j}t - n)\}$.

2.3.3 Discrete-time Wavelet Transform (DTWT)

The discrete-time wavelet transform (DTWT) cannot be obtained by sampling the continuous-time wavelet transforms nor by simply mimicking the continuous ones. Assuming a discrete "mother wavelet" $v(n)$, a discrete-time version of dilation $v(2^k n - m)$ does not produce a frequency response $\sim V(e^{2^k \omega})$. Moreover, a dilation $V(e^{2^k \omega})$ in frequency domain is generally not a band-pass function but a multi-band function. The fundamental difference lies on both the 2π-periodic characteristic of frequency response and the indexing constraint of discrete-time series.

A fast algorithm based on the concept of multiresolution was found by S. Mallat [42] and is illustrated in Figure 2.2.

If we consider only one level, we have

$$d_0(n) = \sum_{m=-\infty}^{\infty} x(m)g(2n - m), \tag{2.6}$$

$$c_0(n) = \sum_{m=-\infty}^{\infty} x(m)h(2n - m), \tag{2.7}$$

$$x(n) = \sum_{l=-\infty}^{\infty} c_0(l)\tilde{h}(n-2l) + \sum_{l=-\infty}^{\infty} d_0(l)\tilde{g}(n-2l). \qquad (2.8)$$

Therefore, the decomposition filters $h(n)$ and $g(n)$ and the reconstruction filters $\tilde{h}(n)$ and $\tilde{g}(n)$ must satisfy:

$$\left.\begin{array}{l} \sum_m g(2n-m)\tilde{g}(m-2l) = \delta(n-l), \\ \sum_m h(2n-m)\tilde{h}(m-2l) = \delta(n-l), \\ \sum_m g(2n-m)\tilde{h}(m-2l) = 0, \\ \sum_m h(2n-m)\tilde{g}(m-2l) = 0, \\ \sum_l h(2l-m)\tilde{h}(n-2l) + \sum_l g(2l-m)\tilde{g}(n-2l) = \delta(m-n) \end{array}\right\} \qquad (2.9)$$

It can be proved (see Appendix A) that in frequency domain those conditions are equivalent to:

$$\left.\begin{array}{l} G(e^{j\omega})\tilde{G}(e^{j\omega}) + G(e^{j(\omega+\pi)})\tilde{G}(e^{j(\omega+\pi)}) = 2 \\ H(e^{j\omega})\widetilde{H}(e^{j\omega}) + H(e^{j(\omega+\pi)})\widetilde{H}(e^{j(\omega+\pi)}) = 2 \\ G(e^{j\omega})\widetilde{H}(e^{j\omega}) + G(e^{j(\omega+\pi)})\widetilde{H}(e^{j(\omega+\pi)}) = 0 \\ H(e^{j\omega})\tilde{G}(e^{j\omega}) + H(e^{j(\omega+\pi)})\tilde{G}(e^{j(\omega+\pi)}) = 0 \\ H(e^{j\omega})\widetilde{H}(e^{j\omega}) + G(e^{j\omega})\tilde{G}(e^{j\omega}) = 2 \\ H(e^{j\omega})\widetilde{H}(e^{j(\omega+\pi)}) + G(e^{j\omega})\tilde{G}(e^{j(\omega+\pi)}) = 0. \end{array}\right\} \qquad (2.10)$$

One possible choice is to choose $h(n)$, $g(n)$, $\tilde{h}(n)$ and $\tilde{g}(n)$ by:

$$\left.\begin{array}{lll} g(n) = (-1)^n h(1-n) & \Leftrightarrow & G(e^{j\omega}) = -e^{-j\omega}H^*(e^{j(\omega+\pi)}), \\ \tilde{h}(n) = h^*(-n) & \Leftrightarrow & \widetilde{H}(e^{j\omega}) = H^*(e^{j\omega}), \\ \tilde{g}(n) = g^*(-n) & \Leftrightarrow & \tilde{G}(e^{j\omega}) = G^*(e^{j\omega}), \end{array}\right\} \qquad (2.11)$$

In this case, the resulting bases is called *orthogonal* bases. Otherwise, the resulting bases is called *biorthogonal* bases.

It can be proved (see Appendix A) that the structure of Figure 2.2 is equivalent to a filter bank with the transform written as [63]:

$$\left.\begin{array}{l} d_k(n) = \displaystyle\sum_{m=-\infty}^{\infty} x(m)v_k(2^{k+1}n - m), \quad 0 \le k \le M-2, \\ c_{M-1}(n) = \displaystyle\sum_{m=-\infty}^{\infty} x(m)v_{M-1}(2^{M-1}n - m), \end{array}\right\} (DTWT)$$

$$x(n) = \sum_{k=0}^{M-2}\sum_{m=-\infty}^{\infty} d_k(m)u_k(n - 2^{k+1}m) + \sum_{m=-\infty}^{\infty} c_{M-1}(m)u_{M-1}(n - 2^{M-1}m)$$
$$(Inverse\ DTWT).$$

Particularly, for orthonomal basis, it can be proved (see Appendix A) that

$$u_k(n) = v_k^*(-n),$$
$$\sum_{m=-\infty}^{\infty} u_k(m - n_k l)u_c^*(m - n_c n) = \delta(k-c)\delta(l-n). \qquad (2.12)$$

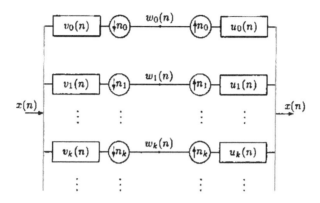

Figure 2.3: Generalized Discrete-time Filter Bank Transform.

Since DTWT can be included into a general framework to be presented next, we leave more in depth discussions to the coming section.

2.4 Generalized Discrete-time Filter Bank Transforms

Previous sections showed that both STFT and DTWT can be implemented by a filter bank structure. If we ignore the modulator $(e^{-j\omega_k n})$ and the demodulator $(e^{j\omega_k n})$ of STFT, the discrete-time version of the two can be included in a generalized form:

$$w_k(n) = \sum_{m=-\infty}^{\infty} x(m)v_k(n_k n - m), \ 0 \le k \le M-1, (GDTFBT) \qquad (2.13)$$

$$x(n) = \sum_{k=0}^{M-1} \sum_{m=-\infty}^{\infty} w_k(m)u_k(n - n_k m) \ (Inverse\ GDTFBT). \qquad (2.14)$$

It was called the *generalized filter bank transform* [63]. Figure 2.3 illustrated the structure of GDTFBT.

Depending on n_k, $v_k(n)$ and $u_k(n)$, GDTFBT includes the following special cases.

1) *Orthonomal wavelet representations.* $n_k = 2^k$ for $0 \le k \le M-2$ and $n_{M-1} = n_{M-2}$. In this case, basis functions possess orthonomality of (2.12).

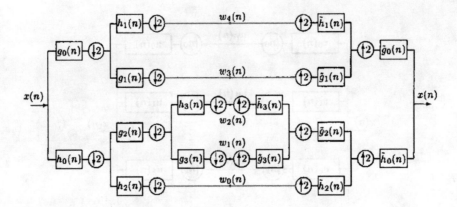

Figure 2.4: Example of General Binary-tree-structured Filter Bank of Five Channels.

2) *Orthonomal wavelet packet representations.* This is a generalization on the orthonomal wavelet by applying the recursive decomposition-reconstruction structure to all branches. Therefore, $n_k = 2^L$ for $0 \leq k \leq 2^L - 1$.

3) *Biorthogonal wavelet (packet) representations.* The same as the *orthonomal* counterpart except that the constraints (2.11) are lifted.

4) *Generalized binary tree structured filter bank representations.* This is a further generalization upon the (bi)orthogonal wavelet (packets). Every channel may be split into two with filters satisfy (2.9). Therefore, every n_k is power of 2. Moreover, filters used in one channel (node) may be different with another. Figure 2.4 showed an example. It was proved in Appendix A that the basis functions constructed this way satisfy the *biorthonomality* expressed by:

$$\sum_{m=-\infty}^{\infty} u_c(m - n_c l) v_k(n_k n - m) = \delta(c - k)\delta(l - n). \qquad (2.15)$$

5) *Overcomplete wavelet representations.* In this case, no down-sampling and up-sampling are used, which means $n_k = 1$ for all channels in the Figure 2.3. As an example, the overcomplete wavelet transform corresponding to Figure 2.4 is shown in Figure 2.5.

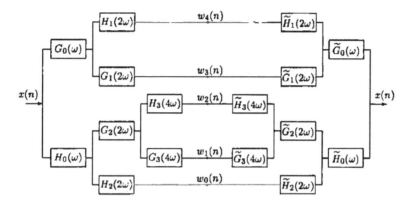

Figure 2.5: The Overcomplete Wavelet Transform for the Example of Figure 2.4.

Representations 1-4 above are called "*complete*". The reason of calling the representations of the category 5 "overcomplete" or "redundant" is that they contain more analyzing functions ($\{u_k(n)\}$) than a basis. Since these analyzing and synthesizing functions must satisfy

$$\sum_{k=0}^{M-1}\sum_{m=-\infty}^{\infty} u_k(m-l)v_k(n-m) = \delta(l-n), \quad or \quad \sum_{k=0}^{M-1} U_k(e^{j\omega})V_k(e^{j\omega}) = 1,$$

they must be *linear dependent*. In the other word, some functions must be expressible by others.

Complete and overcomplete representations behave rather differently under a convolution operator.

2.4.1 Convolution Operator on Complete Representations

In general, a basis function $u_k(n-n_k m)$ is not an eigenfunction of a convolution operator. Using the same idea as in the case of DWT, a convolution operator T_f can be represented by basis functions $\{u_k(n-n_k m)\}$:

$$T_f[u_k(n-n_k m)] = \sum_{c=0}^{M-1}\sum_{b=-\infty}^{\infty} \eta_{k,c}(m,b)u_c(n-n_c b) \, ,$$

$$\eta_{k,c}(m,b) = \sum_{l=-\infty}^{\infty}\sum_{i=-\infty}^{\infty} f(i)u_k(l-i-n_k m)v_c(n_c b-l). \tag{2.16}$$

It can be proved that $u_k(n-n_k m)$ is an eigenfunction of the operator T_f if and only if $\eta_{k,c}(m,b) = \lambda\delta(k-c)\delta(m-b)$.

Proof: If $\eta_{k,c}(m,b) = \lambda\delta(k-c)\delta(m-b)$, then

$$
\begin{aligned}
T_f\left[u_k(n - n_k m)\right] &= \sum_{c=0}^{M-1}\sum_{b=-\infty}^{\infty}\lambda\delta(k-c)\delta(m-b)u_c(n - n_c b) \\
&= \lambda u_k(n - n_k m).
\end{aligned}
$$

In the other direction, if $T_f\left[u_k(n - n_k m)\right] = \lambda u_k(n - n_k m)$, then

$$
\begin{aligned}
\eta_{k,c}(m,b) &= \sum_{n=-\infty}^{\infty} T_f\left[u_k(n - n_k m)\right] v_c(n_c b - n) \\
&= \sum_{n=-\infty}^{\infty} \lambda u_k(n - n_k m) v_c(n_c b - n) = \lambda\delta(k-c)\delta(m-b) \, ,
\end{aligned}
$$

where we utilized the property (2.15). $\blacksquare$

The set of coefficients $\{\eta_{k,c}(m,b)\}$ is the representation of the operator T_f in the basis and is independent of input signal. Since a convolution operation on a sequence $x(n)$ can be derived as:

$$
\begin{aligned}
T_f\left[x(n)\right] &= \sum_{k=0}^{M-1}\sum_{m=-\infty}^{\infty} w_k(m) T_f\left[u_k(n - n_k m)\right] \\
&= \sum_{k=0}^{M-1}\sum_{m=-\infty}^{\infty} w_k(m) \sum_{c=0}^{M-1}\sum_{b=-\infty}^{\infty} \eta_{k,c}(m,b) u_c(n - n_c b) \\
&= \sum_{c=0}^{M-1}\sum_{b=-\infty}^{\infty}\left[\sum_{k=0}^{M-1}\sum_{m=-\infty}^{\infty} w_k(m)\eta_{k,c}(m,b)\right] u_c(n - n_c b) \, ,
\end{aligned}
$$

the representation of $T\left[x(n)\right]$ is thus

$$
\alpha_c(b) = \sum_{k=0}^{M-1}\sum_{m=-\infty}^{\infty} w_k(m)\eta_{k,c}(m,b). \tag{2.17}
$$

For N-periodic sequences $x(n)$, $u_k(n)$ and $v_k(n)$, $\eta_{k,c}(m,b)$ is $\frac{N}{n_k}$-periodic in m index and $\frac{N}{n_c}$-periodic in b index, and $\alpha_c(b)$ is $\frac{N}{n_c}$-periodic in b index.

A representation in matrix form was derived by Banham *et al* [3].

For a translation operator of $f(i) = \delta(i - d)$,

$$
\eta_{k,c}(m,b) = \sum_{l=-\infty}^{\infty} u_k(l - d - n_k m) v_c(n_c b - l),
$$

and generally is not equal to $\lambda\delta(k-c)\delta(m-b)$. Therefore, complete representations are *not* translation invariant.

2.4.2 Convolution Operator on Overcomplete Representations

The overcomplete representation of a convolution operator T_f can be obtained from (2.16) with $n_c = 1$ and $n_k = 1$:

$$\eta_{k,c}(m,b) = \sum_{l=-\infty}^{\infty} \sum_{i=-\infty}^{\infty} f(i)u_k(l-i-m)v_c(b-l) = (f * u_k * v_c)(b-m). \quad (2.18)$$

Accordingly, the overcomplete representation of $T_f[x(n)]$ can be obtained from (2.17):

$$\alpha_c(n) = \sum_{k=0}^{M-1} \sum_{m=-\infty}^{\infty} w_k(m)\eta_{k,c}(n-m) = f(n) * w_c(n), \quad (2.19)$$

which showed that discrete overcomplete wavelet transform operator and convolution operator are commutable, and thus overcomplete wavelet representations are translation-invariant. To verify this, assume an overcomplete wavelet transform operator of $\mathcal{W}$ and a translation operator of T_f with $f(n) = \delta(n-d)$, overcomplete wavelet representation of $T_f[x(n)]$ is:

$$\mathcal{W}T_f[x(n)] = T_f\mathcal{W}[x(n)] = T_f[\{w_k(n)|_{0 \leq k \leq M-1}\}] = \{w_k(n-d)|_{0 \leq k \leq M-1}\},$$

which means that the representation of a time-shifted signal is simply the translated version of the original representation with the same amount of time-shift.

2.4.3 Approximation of Convolution Operators on Overcomplete Representations

In frequency domain, (2.18) can be written as:

$$\hat{\eta}_{k,c}(e^{j\omega}) = F(e^{j\omega})U_k(e^{j\omega})V_c(e^{j\omega}) ,$$

where $\hat{\eta}_{k,c}(e^{j\omega})$ is the discrete-time Fourier transform of $\eta_{k,c}(n)$.

If the passbands of the filters $U_k(e^{j\omega})$ and $V_c(e^{j\omega})$ have little overlap, the following approximation is justified:

$$U_k(e^{j\omega})V_c(e^{j\omega}) \approx \delta(k-c)U_c(e^{j\omega})V_c(e^{j\omega}) .$$

Moreover, if the function $F(e^{j\omega})$ is *real* and the passbands of channel c's are narrow enough, we may further approximate $\hat{\eta}_{k,c}(e^{j\omega})$ as:

$$\hat{\eta}_{k,c}(e^{j\omega}) \approx \lambda_c \delta(k-c) U_c(e^{j\omega}) V_c'(e^{j\omega}),$$

or,

$$\eta_{k,c}(n) \approx \lambda_c \delta(k-c) u_c(n) * v_c(n),$$

where λ_c is a real number. In this case, (2.19) may be well approximated by:

$$\alpha_c(n) \approx \sum_{k=0}^{M-1} \lambda_c \delta(k-c) w_k(n) * u_c(n) * v_c(n) = \lambda_c w_c(n). \tag{2.20}$$

This means that a convolution operator with *real* frequency response $F(e^{j\omega})$ may be approximated by a set of real multipliers $\{\lambda_k\}$. This is another advantage of overcomplete representation since we found that the approximation is generally not extendible to complete representations.

2.4.4 Aliasing Enhancement on Complete Representations

For complete representations, subsampling usually does not meet the Shannon sampling theorem, and thus produces aliasing distortions. Those aliasing components get canceled only by specially designed filters at the reconstruction stage. If we manipulate the representation in a way like (2.20), aliasing distortions may not be canceled. For a concrete example, we consider a wavelet transform of Figure 2.2 with only one level. If we multiply representations $d_0(n)$ and $c_0(n)$ by k_d and k_c respectively, we can rewrite Equations (2.6-2.8) in frequency domain:

$$D_0'(e^{j\omega}) = \frac{1}{2}k_d\left[X(e^{j\omega/2})G(e^{j\omega/2}) + X(e^{j(\omega+2\pi)/2})G(e^{j(\omega+2\pi)/2})\right],$$

$$C_0'(e^{j\omega}) = \frac{1}{2}k_c\left[X(e^{j\omega/2})H(e^{j\omega/2}) + X(e^{j(\omega+2\pi)/2})H(e^{j(\omega+2\pi)/2})\right],$$

$$X'(e^{j\omega}) = \frac{1}{2}\left[k_d G(e^{j\omega})\widetilde{G}(e^{j\omega}) + k_c H(e^{j\omega})\widetilde{H}(e^{j\omega})\right] X(e^{j\omega}) +$$
$$\frac{1}{2}\left[k_d G(e^{j(\omega+\pi)})\widetilde{G}(e^{j\omega}) + k_c H(e^{j(\omega+\pi)})\widetilde{H}(e^{j\omega})\right] X(e^{j(\omega+\pi)}).$$

The second term is the aliasing component. Unless $k_d = k_c$, the second term is generally not equal to zero even though filters meet the perfect reconstruction conditions (2.10). In this case, the system is *not* a linear time invariant (LTI) system, but rather a linear periodically time varying (LPTV) system [63]. It is easy to recognize that the system can not be characterized by the familiar form of $Y(e^{j\omega}) = M(e^{j\omega})X(e^{j\omega})$. Figure 2.6 shows an example of such aliasing-enhancement effect.

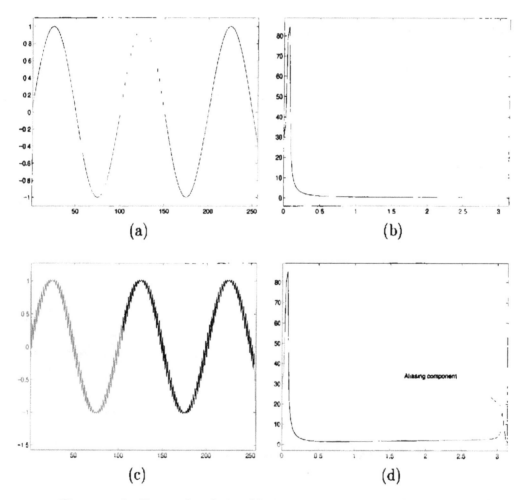

Figure 2.6: Example of the Aliasing-enhancement Anomaly. Where:

    (a) The original sinusoid signal;

    (b) Magnitude of DFT of the signal (a);

    (c) Reconstructed signal with orthogonal Haar filters $(H(e^{j\omega}) = 2^{-1/2}(1 + e^{-j\omega}),\quad G(e^{j\omega}) = 2^{-1/2}(1 - e^{-j\omega}))$, one level decomposition and $k_d = 6$, $k_c = 1$;

    (d) Magnitude of DFT of the signal (c).

2.5   Summary and Discussion

We have reviewed signal representations based on Fourier and wavelet transformations and included them in a general framework called generalized filter bank transform. We studied their behavior under a convolution operator. It revealed that complex sinusoid functions of Fourier transform are the only basis functions in this class which are eigenfunctions of the operator. In this case, a convolution operator is equivalent to multiplications in the representation (frequency) domain and the inverse operator can be simply expressed as divisions. For overcomplete representations, a convolution operator may be approximated by multiplications of coefficients by real factors. However, such an approximation can not be extended to complete representations due to aliasing distortions. Moreover, we realized that discrete complete representations also lack translation-invariant. Based on the characteristics of these representations, we may find the best applications for them.

1) Complete representations may be good for compression, progressive transmission. No redundancy alone would be a major advantage for those applications. Throwing away some coefficients may be seen as a zeroing operation, which does not enhance aliasing components. After all, we are prepared to accept some distortions for those applications.

2) Overcomplete representations possess many desirable properties for restoration, enhancement, feature extraction and time delay estimation [52]. First, they are translation invariant which is critical for pattern recognition. Second, they do not have the aliasing distortions. Third, they allow much higher degree of flexibility in filter design.

CHAPTER 3
OVERCOMPLETE WAVELET REPRESENTATIONS

3.1 Introduction

The paradigm of overcomplete wavelet representations is a versatile and powerful tool shown to be advantageous for certain applications. In this chapter, we shall study overcomplete wavelet representations in detail, including issues of decomposition and reconstruction algorithm, filter selection and time-frequency interpretation.

3.2 Overcomplete Wavelet Transforms and Filters

In general, a discrete-time overcomplete wavelet transform (DTOWT) pair can be obtained by setting n_k to 1 in the Equations (2.13-2.14), as rewritten in the following:

$$w_k(n) = \sum_{m=-\infty}^{\infty} v_k(m)x(n-m), \ 0 \leq k \leq M-1, (DTOWT) \qquad (3.1)$$

$$x(n) = \sum_{k=0}^{M-1} \sum_{m=-\infty}^{\infty} w_k(m)u_k(n-m) \ (Inverse \ DTOWT). \qquad (3.2)$$

More importantly, we need an algorithm to generate analyzing and synthesizing filters $v_k(n)$ and $u_k(n)$. In this thesis, we restrict ourselves to the binary tree algorithm as illustrated in the previous chapter, and consider two particular classes: overcomplete wavelet packets and dyadic wavelets.

3.2.1 Overcomplete Wavelet Packet Representations

The construction algorithm of overcomplete wavelet packet representations corresponds to a complete binary tree, as shown in Figure 3.1. Though each tree node represents an analyzing filter, only a subset of all tree nodes is needed to achieve a perfect reconstruction. Notice that the position and the width of each rectangular

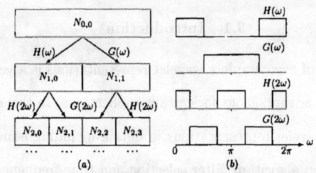

Figure 3.1: Binary Tree for Overcomplete Wavelet Packet Decomposition:
(a) the tree; (b) illustration of frequency scaling of the prototype filters.

node also represents the channel's position and the band width in the frequency domain.

In general, prototype filters $H(\omega)$ and $G(\omega)$ in each level can be distinct, as proved in Appendix A, as long as they satisfy the condition $H(\omega)\widetilde{H}(\omega)+G(\omega)\widetilde{G}(\omega)=1$. The frequency response of each node can be calculated recursively:

$$P_0(\omega) = H(\omega), \quad P_1(\omega) = G(\omega);$$

$$N_{0,0}(\omega) \equiv 1; \quad N_{l+1,m}(\omega) = P_c(2^l\omega)N_{l,\lfloor m/2 \rfloor}(\omega), \quad l \geq 0. \tag{3.3}$$

where the subscript c of the filter $P_c(\omega)$ follows the periodic pattern of $0, 1, 1, 0$, and can be calculated by:

$$c = (m + \lfloor m/2 \rfloor) \bmod 2.$$

The purpose of such ordering is to make the index m of the node $N_{l,m}$ proportional to its central frequency.

The reconstruction from two child nodes to their parent node can be expressed by the following formula:

$$N_{l+1,2k}(\omega)\widetilde{P}_{k\bmod 2}(2^l\omega) + N_{l+1,2k+1}(\omega)\widetilde{P}_{(k+1)\bmod 2}(2^l\omega) = N_{l,k}(\omega),$$

where we used the property of:

$$P_{k\bmod 2}(\omega)\widetilde{P}_{k\bmod 2}(\omega) + P_{(k+1)\bmod 2}(\omega)\widetilde{P}_{(k+1)\bmod 2}(\omega)$$

$$= H(\omega)\widetilde{H}(\omega) + G(\omega)\widetilde{G}(\omega) = 1.$$

There are many possible choices of filters $v_k(n)$ from the tree to achieve the perfect reconstruction. For example, for the tree shown in the Figure 3.1 with the height of two [55, page 449], five sets are available: $\{N_{0,0}\}$, $\{N_{1,0}, N_{1,1}\}$, $\{N_{1,0}, N_{2,2}, N_{2,3}\}$, $\{N_{2,0}, N_{2,1}, N_{1,1}\}$ and $\{N_{2,0}, N_{2,1}, N_{2,2}, N_{2,3}\}$. In general, let $T(h)$ be the number of selections from a complete binary decomposition tree of height h. Since the tree may be split into two subtrees of height $h-1$ each in turn have $T(h-1)$ selections, we have the following recursive formula:

$$T(h) = [T(h-1)]^2 + 1, \; h \geq 1, \; and \; T(0) = 1.$$

The first five numbers were calculated as $T(1)=2$, $T(2)=5$, $T(3)=26$, $T(4)=677$ and $T(5)=458330$.

All quadrature mirror filters (QMF), good for orthogonal wavelet transform, are also good for overcomplete wavelet packet transforms. However, for *real* QMF except Haar wavelet, I. Daubechies proved that linear phase and finite impulse response (FIR) properties are mutual exclusive [13]. For example, Daubechies wavelet filters [11] are FIR but not linear phase. In the other hand, Battle-Lemarié wavelet filters are symmetric but not FIR, which may be written as [42]:

$$H_p(\omega) = \sqrt{\frac{\Sigma_{4p+4}(\omega)}{2^{4p+4}\Sigma_{4p+4}(2\omega)}} \tag{3.4}$$

where p is a positive integer and

$$\Sigma_n(\omega) = \sum_{k=-\infty}^{+\infty} \frac{1}{(\omega + 2k\pi)^n}.$$

Note: An algorithm for numerical computation of Battle-Lemarié wavelets is included in Appendix B.

3.2.2 Dyadic Wavelet Representations

The building structure of a dyadic wavelet transform is a particular subset of the overcomplete wavelet packet transform. It decomposes low-frequency branch only (assume $H(\omega)$ is lowpass), as shown in Figure 3.2.

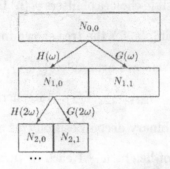

Figure 3.2: Binary Tree for Dyadic Wavelet Decomposition.

Obviously, all filters good for overcomplete wavelet packet transforms are good for dyadic wavelet transforms. However, one may want to exploit the extra opportunity created by the more relaxed constraint on filters. The following filter classes [44, 20] possess distinct property in the time domain:

$$\begin{aligned}
H(\omega) &= e^{jp\omega/2}\cos^{2n+p}(\omega/2), \\
\widetilde{H}(\omega) &= H^*(\omega), \\
G(\omega) &= -(-j)^p e^{-jp\omega/2}\sin^{2-p}(\omega/2), \\
\tilde{G}(\omega) &= -(j)^p e^{jp\omega/2}\sin^p(\omega/2)\sum_{m=0}^{2n+p-1}\cos^{2m}(\omega/2)
\end{aligned}$$

(3.5)

where $n > 0$ is an integer and $p \in \{0, 1\}$.

In fact, for: $p = 0$ filter $g(-1) = 0.25$, $g(0) = -0.5$ and $g(1) = 0.25$ is proportional to a discrete Laplacian operator and for: $p = 1$, $g(0) = 0.5$ and $g(1) = -0.5$ is proportional to a discrete gradient operator.

Notice that filters within this class are linear phase and FIR, but not orthogonal. For $p = 0$, filters H, $\widetilde{H}$, G and $\tilde{G}$ and their frequency scalings (e.g. $H(2^l\omega)$) are all symmetric. For $p = 1$, different prototype filters may be used for frequency scaling to minimize spatial shifting caused by the phase factor. If we denote $H_l(\omega)$, $\widetilde{H}_l(\omega)$, $G_l(\omega)$ and $\tilde{G}_l(\omega)$ for filters used in level $l > 1$, we find the following filters are either symmetric or antisymmetric as well as FIR:

$$\begin{aligned}
H_l(\omega) &= \cos^{2n+1}(2^{l-2}\omega), \quad \widetilde{H}_l(\omega) = H_l(\omega), \\
G_l(\omega) &= j\sin(2^{l-2}\omega), \qquad \tilde{G}_l(\omega) = -G_l(\omega)\sum_{m=0}^{2n}\cos^{2m}(2^{l-2}\omega).
\end{aligned}$$

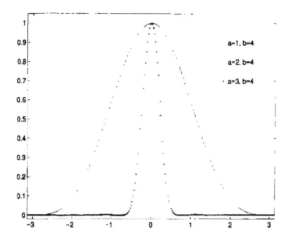

Figure 3.3: Examples of the Function $\Theta_{a,b}(\omega)$.

In both cases, frequency response of tree node $N_{l,k}$ ($l > 0$ and $k \in \{0,1\}$) can be derived as:

$$N_{l,0}(\omega) = e^{jp\omega/2} \prod_{m=0}^{l-1} \cos^{2n+p}(2^{m-1}\omega) = e^{jp\omega/2} \left[\frac{\sin(2^{l-1}\omega)}{2^l \sin(\omega/2)}\right]^{2n+p},$$

$$N_{l,1}(\omega) = -(-j)^p e^{-jp\omega/2} \left[2^{l-1}\sin(\omega/2)\right]^{2-p} \left[\frac{\sin(2^{l-2}\omega)}{2^{l-1}\sin(\omega/2)}\right]^{2n+2}.$$

For convenience, we defined a function $\Theta_{a,b}(\omega)$ as:

$$\Theta_{a,b}(\omega) = \left[\frac{\sin(2^{a-1}\omega)}{2^a \sin(\omega/2)}\right]^b.$$

For $b \geq 4$, the function $\Theta_{a,b}(\omega)$ is approximately Gaussian as plotted in Figure 3.3.

Similarly, we can define a reconstruction tree with nodes:

$$\widetilde{N}_{l,0}(\omega) = \prod_{m=1}^{l} \widetilde{H}_m(\omega),$$
$$\widetilde{N}_{l,1}(\omega) = \widetilde{N}_{l-1,0}(\omega)\widetilde{G}_l(\omega).$$

A dyadic wavelet representation consists of leaf nodes. For example, a three-level representation consists of nodes $\{N_{3,0}, N_{3,1}, N_{2,1}, N_{1,1}\}$. In terms of filter bank, they can be viewed as multiple channels. Channel frequency responses can be derived as:

$$C_{l,0}(\omega) = N_{l,0}(\omega)\widetilde{N}_{l,0}(\omega) = \prod_{m=1}^{l} H_m(\omega)\widetilde{H}_m(\omega) = \Theta_{l,4n+2p}(\omega),$$

$$C_{l,1}(\omega) = N_{l,1}(\omega)\widetilde{N}_{l,1}(\omega) = N_{l-1,0}(\omega)\widetilde{N}_{l-1,0}(\omega)G_l(\omega)\widetilde{G}_l(\omega)$$

$$
\begin{aligned}
&= N_{l-1,0}(\omega)\widetilde{N}_{l-1,0}(\omega)\left[1 - H_l(\omega)\widetilde{H}_l(\omega)\right] \\
&= \Theta_{l-1,4n+2p}(\omega) - \Theta_{l,4n+2p}(\omega).
\end{aligned}
$$

The channel frequency responses for a three-level representation are $\{C_{3,0}, C_{3,1}, C_{2,1}, C_{1,1}\}$. Notice that the channel frequency responses $C_{l,1}(\omega)$ are an approximate difference of two Gaussians (DOG) [47, page 63]. Two examples of channel filters are shown in Figure 3.6.

3.2.3 Filters of Autocorrelation Functions of Wavelets

From a filtering point of view, the idea is very simple. Since there is no downsampling-upsampling taking place in overcomplete wavelet transforms, it seems that we can simply combine decomposition and reconstruction into a single filtering step. To achieve this, one only need to change prototype filters into:

$$
\begin{aligned}
H_a(\omega) &= H(\omega)\widetilde{H}(\omega), \\
G_a(\omega) &= G(\omega)\widetilde{G}(\omega).
\end{aligned}
\tag{3.6}
$$

The perfect reconstruction condition now takes the form of:

$$
H_a(\omega) + G_a(\omega) = 1.
$$

As $H(\omega)$ is connected to a wavelet, $H_a(\omega)$ is connected to an autocorrelation function of wavelet. For rigorous mathematical treatment, refer to Saito's Ph.D thesis [57].

In this case, a reconstruction step is simply a summation of all coefficients as (3.2) degenerates to:

$$
x(n) = \sum_{k=0}^{M-1} w_k(n),
$$

which takes the same form as the generalized STFT.

The most important property is that filters $H_a(\omega)$ and $G_a(\omega)$ are always symmetric or antisymmetric, and thus providing a simple way to construct symmetry and FIR filters for certain applications.

3.3 Connection to Complete Wavelet Representations

In Appendix A, Proposition A.0.3 built the bridge between an overcomplete wavelet representation and a complete wavelet representation. If both representations used the exactly same prototype filters $H(\omega)$, $G(\omega)$, $\widetilde{H}(\omega)$ and $\widetilde{G}(\omega)$, the only difference lies on the decimation. In this case, the complete wavelet representation is a subset of the corresponding overcomplete wavelet representation due to decimation. If the prototype filters used by an overcomplete wavelet representation does not satisfy (2.10), there is no corresponding complete wavelet representation.

3.4 Time-frequency Interpretation and the Uncertainty Principle

The set of transform coefficients $\{w_k(n)|_{0 \leq k \leq M-1}\}$ is a representation of the signal $x(n)$ in the transform domain. It is important to point out that an analyzing filter $V_k(\omega)$ with nonzero phase response will cause a time shift [49, page 205] d_k in the corresponding component $w_k(n)$. For some applications, e.g., segmentation, this shift has to be compensated. In this case, $\{w_k(n + d_k)|_{0 \leq k \leq M-1}\}$ should be used as the representation.

Figure 3.4 shows two overcomplete wavelet packet representations using symmetric Lemarié filter of $p = 1$. It is apparent that overcomplete wavelet representations include both frequency and temporal information of the signals. The frequency resolution or capability to separate different frequency component of an overcomplete wavelet representation is determined by $V_k(\omega)$'s. The narrower the passband of the $V_k(\omega)$ is, the higher it is the frequency resolution. On the other hand, the time resolution is determined by the distribution (or window size) of the impulse responses $v_k(n)$'s. The shorter the distribution is, the higher the time resolution it can achieve. Unfortunately, high resolution in time and frequency domains are conflict goals, as demonstrated in the Figure 3.5. In this example, we saw that as passband narrowed, impulse responses spread and consequently the boundary between

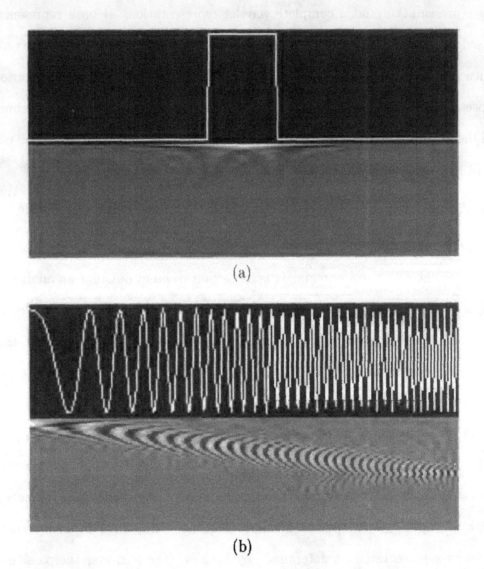

(a)

(b)

Figure 3.4: Two Examples of the Overcomplete Wavelet Representation.
Legend:

(a) An ideal square waveform;

(b) A linear chirp signal $s(n) = 5\cos(0.02\pi n + 0.001\pi n^2)$.

In each image, top half is the signal waveform, and the bottom
half is (0-255) scaled overcomplete wavelet representation (coefficients) of 64 leaf nodes of the level six. For the bottom half,
horizontal axis is time, vertical axis is frequency.

two impulses blurred. This phenomenon reflected a fundamental principle called the *uncertainty principle* [21, 51].

Time and frequency localization of a discrete *lowpass* function $f(n)$ can be mathematically described by two quantities,

$$\sigma_n^2 = \frac{1}{E} \sum_n (n - \bar{n})^2 |f(n)|^2,$$

$$\sigma_\omega^2 = \frac{1}{2\pi E} \int_{-\pi}^{\pi} \omega^2 |F(e^{j\omega})|^2 d\omega,$$

where $E = \sum_n |f(n)|^2 = \frac{1}{2\pi} \int_{-\pi}^{\pi} |F(e^{j\omega})|^2 d\omega$, and $\bar{n} = \frac{1}{E} \sum_n n|f(n)|^2$.

The product of σ_n^2 and σ_ω^2 is defined as the *uncertainty factor*:

$$U = \sigma_n^2 \sigma_\omega^2. \tag{3.7}$$

Liu and Akansu [40] proved that $U \geq \left[E - |F(e^{j\pi})|^2 \right] / (4E^2)$, and thus for filters with $F(e^{j\pi}) = 0$, $U \geq 0.25$. That the uncertainty factor has a lower bound is significant and is called the *uncertainty principle*. It basically states that we cannot have filters with arbitrarily narrow bandwidth in the frequency domain and arbitrarily short duration in the time domain. As a result, we cannot achieve arbitrarily precise time and frequency localization simultaneously. (Numerical computation of uncertainty factors for filter banks is discussed in Appendix C.)

Figure 3.6 shows examples of analyzing filters of overcomplete wavelet transform and their uncertainty factors. Uncertainty factors of the analyzing filters of the dyadic wavelet showed that they are indeed very close to Gaussian functions. In general, the results showed that uncertainty factor varied from channel to channel, and level to level. As a statistical measure, we used maximum, minimum and mean to describe higher levels. Such statistics for higher level overcomplete wavelet packets are presented in the Table 3.1, where *Regular* stands for regular Lemarié filters of (3.4) and *Autocorrelation* stands for autocorrelation functions of Lemarié filters.

We may catch some trends from the data on Lemarié-filter-spanned analyzing filters of overcomplete wavelet packet representations:

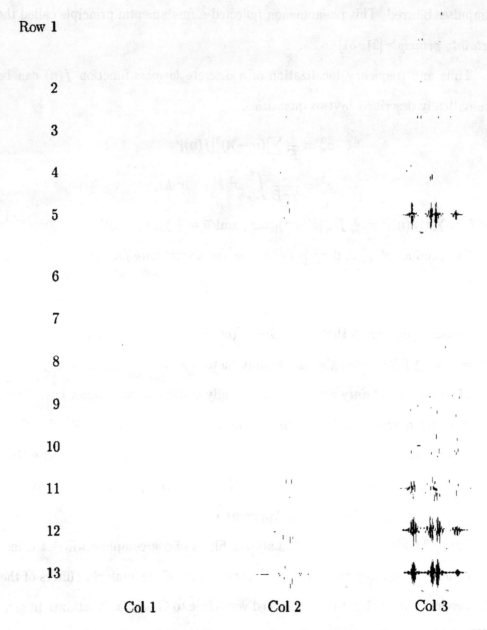

Figure 3.5: Examples of Time-frequency Localization by Overcomplete Wavelet Packet Representations.

Where:

Row 1: A signal consists of two pure-tone impulses with frequency of $\omega = 0.3\pi$ and $\omega = 0.32\pi$: the spectral (Col 1) and the waveform (Col 3).

Row 2-5: level 2 representation.

Row 6-13: level 3 representation.

For row 2-13: column1, frequency responses $\{N_{l,k}|0 \leq k \leq 2^l\}$; column2, impulse responses of column1 (dot lines approximate envelopes). column3, overcomplete wavelet representation. The prototype filter used was Lemaré filter of $p = 1$.

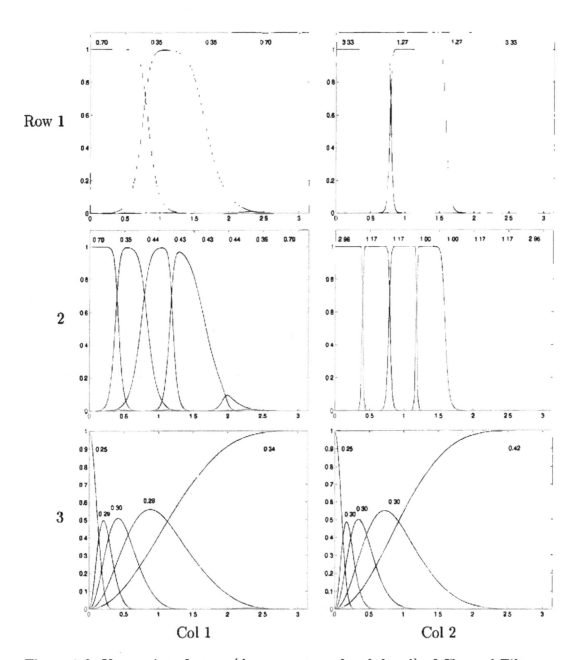

Row 1

2

3

Col 1

Col 2

Figure 3.6: Uncertainty factors (drawn on top of each band) of Channel Filters. Where:

Row 1: Overcomplete wavelet packet of level 2 using Lemarié filter of $p = 1$ (Col 1) and $p = 9$ (Col 2);

Row 2: Overcomplete wavelet packet of level 3 using Lemarié filter of $p = 1$ (Col 1) and $p = 9$ (Col 2);

Row 3: Channel filters $\{C_{4,0}, C_{4,1}, C_{3,1}, C_{2,1}, C_{1,1}\}$ of dyadic wavelet using the filter class of (3.5) with $n = 1$ (Col 1) and $p = 1$, $n = 1$ (Col 2).

Table 3.1: Uncertainty Factors of Analyzing Filters

p	level	Regular			Autocorrelation		
		U_{max}	U_{min}	$\overline{U}$	U_{max}	U_{min}	$\overline{U}$
	4	1.618	0.350	0.701	0.853	0.367	0.497
1	5	5.581	0.342	1.705	2.053	0.318	0.579
	6	16.721	0.318	4.535	5.693	0.262	0.980
	4	1.011	0.437	0.628	1.178	0.470	0.584
2	5	3.464	0.397	0.954	0.871	0.333	0.432
	6	7.984	0.320	1.809	2.736	0.260	0.475
	4	1.283	0.529	0.674	1.349	0.496	0.646
3	5	2.386	0.418	0.704	0.721	0.329	0.398
	6	5.244	0.318	1.005	1.605	0.261	0.346

1) Joint time-frequency localization of those using low order filters tends to deteriorate quickly as level increase. This is due to the existence of small sidelobes.

2) Using filters of autocorrelation function is more effective than using higher order regular filter, if the no-reconstruction structure is acceptable by applications.

However, one should be very careful in using uncertainty factors as an optimality measure due to two main reasons. First, how can we come up a single sensible number for a filter bank? Minimum U_{max} or minimum $\overline{U}$ or something else? Second, more fundamentally, the uncertainty factor does not take the signal into account. For configurations with similar uncertainty factors, as in the case of Gaussian-like filters such as (3.5), the measure of uncertainty factor alone would not tell us which one is optimal.

3.5 Two-dimensional Extensions

So far we have only discussed one-dimensional representations. In order to apply overcomplete wavelet transforms to two-dimensional images, we need to extend the transform to two-dimension. The following two separable extensions can be implemented as separated 1D filtering of rows and columns.

1) *Tensor product extension* [42]. This extension is originally applied to orthogonal wavelet transform. Only 1D filters $H(\omega)$ and $G(\omega)$ are used. It directly exploit the perfect reconstruction property of quadrature mirror filters by extending:

$$H(\omega)\widetilde{H}(\omega) + G(\omega)\tilde{G}(\omega) = 1$$

into:

$$\left[H(\omega_x)\widetilde{H}(\omega_x) + G(\omega_x)\tilde{G}(\omega_x)\right]\left[H(\omega_y)\widetilde{H}(\omega_y) + G(\omega_y)\tilde{G}(\omega_y)\right] = 1.$$

The above 2D extension can be rewritten as

$$HH(\omega_x,\omega_y)\widetilde{HH}(\omega_x,\omega_y) + HG(\omega_x,\omega_y)\widetilde{HG}(\omega_x,\omega_y)$$
$$+$$
$$GH(\omega_x,\omega_y)\widetilde{GH}(\omega_x,\omega_y) + GG(\omega_x,\omega_y)\widetilde{GG}(\omega_x,\omega_y) = 1,$$

where

$$
\begin{aligned}
HH(\omega_x,\omega_y) &= H(\omega_x)H(\omega_y), & \widetilde{HH}(\omega_x,\omega_y) &= \widetilde{H}(\omega_x)\widetilde{H}(\omega_y), \\
HG(\omega_x,\omega_y) &= H(\omega_x)G(\omega_y), & \widetilde{HG}(\omega_x,\omega_y) &= \widetilde{H}(\omega_x)\tilde{G}(\omega_y), \\
GH(\omega_x,\omega_y) &= G(\omega_x)H(\omega_y), & \widetilde{GH}(\omega_x,\omega_y) &= \tilde{G}(\omega_x)\widetilde{H}(\omega_y), \\
GG(\omega_x,\omega_y) &= G(\omega_x)G(\omega_y), & \widetilde{GG}(\omega_x,\omega_y) &= \tilde{G}(\omega_x)\tilde{G}(\omega_y).
\end{aligned}
$$

Filters $\{HH, HG, GH, GG\}$ are used for decomposition while filters $\{\widetilde{HH}, \widetilde{HG}, \widetilde{GH}, \widetilde{GG}\}$ are used for reconstruction. The same construction method is applied to frequency scaling of higher levels with each node decomposed into four child nodes.

2) *Two-orientational extension.* For the particular dyadic wavelet filters (3.5) with emphasis on spatial operation (gradient and Laplacian), the component $\{GG\}$ of the tensor product method may not be useful. Therefore, the following 2D extension was proposed by Mallat [44]:

$$
\begin{aligned}
HH(\omega_x,\omega_y) &= H(\omega_x)H(\omega_y), & \widetilde{HH}(\omega_x,\omega_y) &= \widetilde{H}(\omega_x)\widetilde{H}(\omega_y), \\
GX(\omega_x,\omega_y) &= G(\omega_x), & \widetilde{GX}(\omega_x,\omega_y) &= \tilde{G}(\omega_x)L(\omega_y), \\
GY(\omega_x,\omega_y) &= G(\omega_y), & \widetilde{GY}(\omega_x,\omega_y) &= L(\omega_x)\tilde{G}(\omega_y).
\end{aligned}
$$

This 2D extension has only three components:

- a horizontal component GX
- a vertical component GY
- a lower resolution component HH

However, it introduced a new filter $L(\omega)$, which is to be determined by the condition of:

$$HH \cdot \widetilde{HH} + GX \cdot \widetilde{GX} + GY \cdot \widetilde{GY} = 1.$$

It turned out that the formula for $L(\omega)$ is

$$L(\omega) = \frac{1 + H(\omega)\widetilde{H}(\omega)}{2}.$$

For filters of (3.5),

$$L(\omega) = 0.5 * \left[1 + \cos^{4n+2p}(\omega/2)\right],$$

which is a symmetric and FIR filter.

CHAPTER 4
OPERATIONS ON OVERCOMPLETE WAVELET REPRESENTATIONS

4.1 Introduction

In most cases, a suitable signal representation is not the end of a problem-solving process. On the contrary, how to manipulate it to achieve a desired effect is the more challenging part.

For overcomplete wavelet representations, we have identified three operations: gain, shrinkage and envelope operators for our applications in image deblurring and segmentation. We demonstrated that a linear convolution may be approximated by a gain operator, and devised a tree pruning algorithm based on a tolerant of approximation error. We extended the wavelet shrinkage proposed by Donoho and Johnstone [17] to overcomplete wavelet representations for denoising. We built the connection between the power density distribution of a overcomplete wavelet representation and its envelopes, and presented two envelope detection algorithms.

4.2 Gain Operators

In the Section 2.4.3, we determined that a convolution operator can be approximated by multiplication of *real* factors $\{\lambda_k|_{0 \le k \le M-1}\}$, followed by a reconstruction. Such a operation can be denoted by a *gain operator* $\mathcal{G}$. When applied to a over-complete wavelet representation, a gain operator $\mathcal{G}$ multiplies $w_k(n)$ by a *real* gain of λ_k. Notice that such gain operators are *linear* and *memoryless*. We called the set of gain factors $\{\lambda_k|_{0 \le k \le M-1}\} \in \Re^M$ a *gain vector*. In fact, such a operation with an *arbitrary* gain vector is equivalent to a linear filtering. For a given channel configuration and a gain vector $\{\lambda_k|_{0 \le k \le M-1}\}$, the relationship between a signal $x(n)$ and the reconstructed signal $x'(n)$ in the frequency domain is simply

$$X'(\omega) = \sum_{k=0}^{M-1} \lambda_k W_k(\omega)U_k(\omega) = X(\omega)\sum_{k=0}^{M-1} \lambda_k V_k(\omega)U_k(\omega),$$

and thus the equivalent filter is

$$Q(\omega) = [\lambda_0\lambda_1\cdots\lambda_{M-1}]\,[C_0(\omega)C_1(\omega)\cdots C_{M-1}(\omega)]^t,$$

where $[\lambda_0\lambda_1\cdots\lambda_{M-1}]$ is a gain vector, $C_k(\omega)=V_k(\omega)U_k(\omega)$ is the channel filters, and M^t denotes the matrix transpose of M.

Two fundamental issues immediately arise:

1) What is the characteristics of the set of filters expressible by a gain operator? In the other words, what kind of filters may be approximated by a gain operator? A broad answer is that any gain operator can only represent a *symmetric* filter. This is because channel filters $\{C_k(\omega)|0\leq k\leq M-1\}$ of overcomplete wavelet representations are usually *real* functions, any linear combination of them must also be a real function.

2) For a given frequency response $F(\omega)$, how can we determine a tree configuration and a gain vector as the best approximation? Note that this question really asks for a criteria of "best" and an algorithm to find it.

4.2.1 Minimum Mean Square Error (MMSE) Approximation

The closeness of the approximation in terms of frequency response by a wavelet representation with channel frequency responses $\{C_k(\omega)|_{0\leq k\leq M-1}\}$ and a gain vector $\{\lambda_k|_{0\leq k\leq M-1}\}$ to a given *real* function $F(\omega)$ may be measured by the following *mean square error*:

$$\delta = \frac{1}{2\pi}\int_{-\pi}^{\pi}\left[F(\omega) - \sum_{k=0}^{M-1}\lambda_k C_k(\omega)\right]^2 d\omega. \tag{4.1}$$

It is well known that the optimal gain vector corresponding to the minimum mean square error may be found by setting all partial derivatives $\frac{\partial \delta}{\partial \lambda_q}$ to zero:

$$\frac{\partial \delta}{\partial \lambda_q} = -\frac{1}{\pi} \int_{-\pi}^{\pi} \left[F(\omega) - \sum_{k=0}^{M-1} \lambda_k C_k(\omega) \right] C_q(\omega) d\omega = 0, \ 0 \leq q \leq M-1,$$

which is a set of linear equations:

$$\sum_{k=0}^{M-1} \left[\int_{-\pi}^{\pi} C_k(\omega) C_q(\omega) d\omega \right] \lambda_k = \int_{-\pi}^{\pi} F(\omega) C_q(\omega) d\omega, \ 0 \leq q \leq M-1. \qquad (4.2)$$

The minimum mean square error can be derived as

$$\delta_{min} = \frac{1}{2\pi} \int_{-\pi}^{\pi} F^2(\omega) d\omega - \sum_{k=0}^{M-1} \lambda_k^o \frac{1}{2\pi} \int_{-\pi}^{\pi} F(\omega) C_k(\omega) d\omega,$$

where $\{\lambda_k^o|_{0 \leq q \leq M-1}\}$ is the optimal gain vector satisfying (4.2).

We may define a *normalized* minimum mean square error (*NMMSE*) ε as

$$\varepsilon = \frac{\delta_{min}}{E_f},$$

where $E_f = \frac{1}{2\pi} \int_{-\pi}^{\pi} F^2(\omega) d\omega$ is the energy of the given frequency response. Since $\delta_{min} \geq 0$, it must be true that

$$E_f \geq \sum_{k=0}^{M-1} \lambda_k^o \frac{1}{2\pi} \int_{-\pi}^{\pi} F(\omega) C_k(\omega) d\omega,$$

and therefore $0 \leq \varepsilon \leq 1$.

The criteria of mean square error provides a way to determine the optimal gain vector for a given frequency response $F(\omega)$ and a given configuration. However, the criteria alone suggests that the bottom-most nodes are the best representation, for which ε may reach its minimum among all possible configurations. This can be formally proved by the following proposition.

Proposition 4.2.1 *Splitting a channel into two will not increase the error measure* ε.

Proof: By contradiction. Assume that for the current configuration $\{C_k(\omega)|_{0 \leq k \leq M-1}\}$, the optimal gain vector is $\{\lambda_k^o\}$ and the *NMMSE* is ε. We further assume that the channel q is split into two channels with indexes q_1 and q_2, with the optimal gain vector $\{\lambda_k^{q'}\}$ for the new configuration and the new $\varepsilon' > \varepsilon$.

Without loss of generality, we can write:

$$
\begin{aligned}
C_{q_1}(\omega) &= C_q(\omega)H(2^l\omega)\widetilde{H}(2^l\omega), \\
C_{q_2}(\omega) &= C_q(\omega)G(2^l\omega)\widetilde{G}(2^l\omega).
\end{aligned} \tag{4.3}
$$

Since the prototype filters satisfy $H(\omega)\widetilde{H}(\omega) + G(\omega)\widetilde{G}(\omega) = 1$, we have $C_{q_1}(\omega) + C_{q_2}(\omega) = C_q(\omega)$. For the new configuration, we can find a gain vector $\{\lambda_k' = \lambda_k^o, k \neq q_1, k \neq q_2; \lambda_{q_1}' = \lambda_{q_2}' = \lambda_q^o\}$ with error $\varepsilon' = \varepsilon$. This contradicts the assumption that $\varepsilon' > \varepsilon$, and therefore $\varepsilon' \leq \varepsilon$ ∎

Examples showing higher level corresponding to better approximation can be visualized in Figure 4.1. Overcomplete wavelet packet representations of leaf nodes at Level 4, 5, 6, 7 were selected, corresponding to 16, 32, 64, 128 channels, respectively. Lemarié filter of $p = 3$ were used.

4.2.2 Time-frequency Trade-off and a Greedy Algorithm

Proposition 4.2.1 clearly states that approximation error ε of frequency response decreases as the channel bandwidth decreases, as demonstrated by the examples in Figure 4.1. Therefore, by the criteria alone, the Fourier transform would be the best representation since its approximation error is zero. This is certainly not the answer we are looking for.

What we lost in sight is the other part of the picture in the time domain. As dictated by the uncertainty principle, time resolution decreased as the frequency resolution increased. A overcomplete wavelet packet representation by the deepest leaves would be closed to a Fourier representation and thus lost its resolution in the time domain. Moreover, from computational point of view, such a down-to-the-bottom decomposition is rather inefficient.

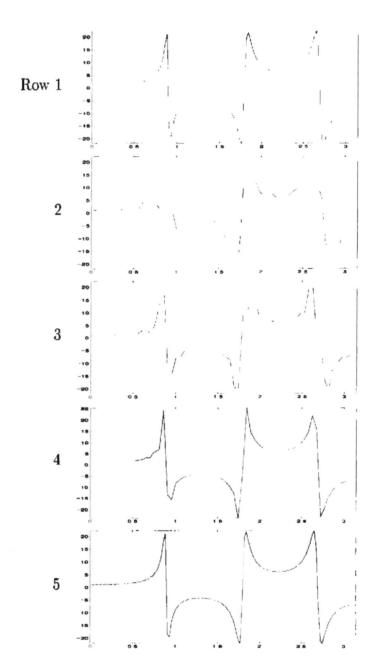

Figure 4.1: Examples of Gain Vector Approximation (frequency range $[0, \pi]$ shown)
Where:

Row 1: a given frequency response $F(e^{j\omega})$;

Row 2 to 5: approximated frequency responses by overcomplete wavelet packet representations of level 4, 5, 6, 7, overlaid with $F(e^{j\omega})$ (dotted curve), with ε=39.4%, 18.5%, 4.5%, 0.02%, respectively.

One possible trade-off between time and frequency can be accomplished by setting up a tolerant on the approximation error ε. Under an error tolerant, the goal could be to find a tree configuration with minimum number of leaves. In the following, we present a greedy algorithm in the order of breadth-first search [45]. Notice that a tree node here represents a channel filter $C_{l,m}(\omega)$ and the relationship between children nodes and their parent node is characterized by (4.3).

Algorithm 4.2.2 (Minimum Tree) *Given a frequency response $F(\omega)$ and an error tolerant ε_0, let current leaves $\mathcal{L} = \{C_{0,0}(\omega) \equiv 1\}$ and compute the current error $\varepsilon_{\mathcal{L}}$ using the set $\mathcal{L}$.*

Step 1. *One by one, compute error ε_k by temporarily substituting a node in the current leaves $\mathcal{L}$ with its two children. Choose the pair with minimum ε_k to replace their parent in the set $\mathcal{L}$ and update the current error $\varepsilon_{\mathcal{L}} = \min\{\varepsilon_k\}$.*

Step 2. *If $\varepsilon_{\mathcal{L}} \leq \varepsilon_0$, stop and use the leaves $\mathcal{L}$ as representation; else, go to step 1.*

Examples of overcomplete wavelet packet approximation using the minimum tree algorithm are shown in Figure 4.2. The improvement is appreciated by comparing it with Figure 4.1. In Figure 4.1, the representation using thirty-two channels of the Level 5 has the approximation error $\varepsilon = 18.5\%$. However, for the same frequency response, the minimum tree algorithm was able to find a representation of only twenty-six channels and yet reduced the approximation error to $\varepsilon = 6\%$. In the other case, the minimum tree algorithm found a representation with merely seven channels and achieved approximation error of 0.6%.

4.3 Shrinking Operators

Wavelet shrinkage was introduced by Donoho and Johnstone [17] for signal denoising and linear inverse problems. For a thorough introduction, refer to [15]. The description of the methodology was given in [15, page 173], we quote, "Wavelet

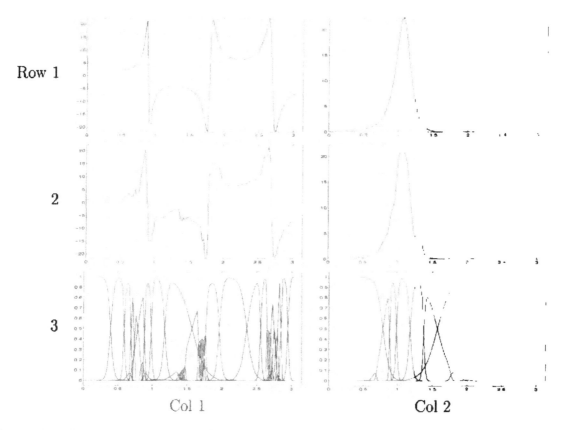

Row 1

2

3

Col 1   Col 2

Figure 4.2: Examples of the Minimum Tree Approximation with the Maximum Depth of Seven Levels.

Where:

Col 1: A given frequency response $F_1(e^{j\omega})$ (row1, same as in Figure 4.1), approximation result overlaid with F_1 (row2) with $\varepsilon = 6\%$ and selected 26 channels (row3);

Col 2: A given frequency response $F_2(e^{j\omega})$ (row1), approximation result overlaid with F_2 (row2) with $\varepsilon = 0.6\%$ and selected 7 channels (row3).

Overcomplete wavelet packet with Lemarié filter $H_1(e^{j\omega})$ was used in both cases, and the frequency range $[0, \pi]$ is shown.

shrinkage refers to reconstructions obtained by wavelet transformation, followed by shrinking the empirical wavelet coefficients towards zero, followed by inverse transformation." For a thorough introduction, refer to [15].

We extended the idea to overcomplete wavelet representations on the ground that they differs with orthogonal wavelet representations mainly on having extra correlated coefficients.

A shrinking operator $\mathcal{K}_t$ can be written as

$$\mathcal{K}_t[w] = \begin{cases} w - t, & w > t, \\ 0, & |w| \le t, \\ w + t, & w < -t, \end{cases} \tag{4.4}$$

where $t > 0$ is a threshold. Notice that the shrinking operator is a *nonlinear* and *memoryless* operator, and is supposed to work in spatial domain.

The goal of a shrinking operation is to cut the noise off while keeping useful signals. Obviously, this is possible only if the amplitude of desirable components is stronger than the noise components. Therefore, the threshold value t is dependent on the signal-to-noise ratio. Examples of choosing appropriate thresholds are discussed in Chapter 6.

To demonstrate the shrinking operation and the advantage of wavelet denoising, an example is included in Figure 4.3. The major advantage of wavelet shrinkage denoising, as compared with linear smoothing, is that it diminishes noise but does not smear the sharp edges, as seen in the example. Comparison with a linear averaging filter with $h = [1, 1, 1, 1, 1, 1, 1]/7$ is presented in Figure 4.4.

4.4 Envelope Detectors

Energy distribution is a very important concept in the physical world. It is a indispensable tool for signal analysis, too.

For a harmonic current $i(t) = A\sin(\omega_0 t + \alpha)$ passing through a one-ohm pure resistant, the instantaneous power (energy per unit time) at time t is $i^2(t)$. The

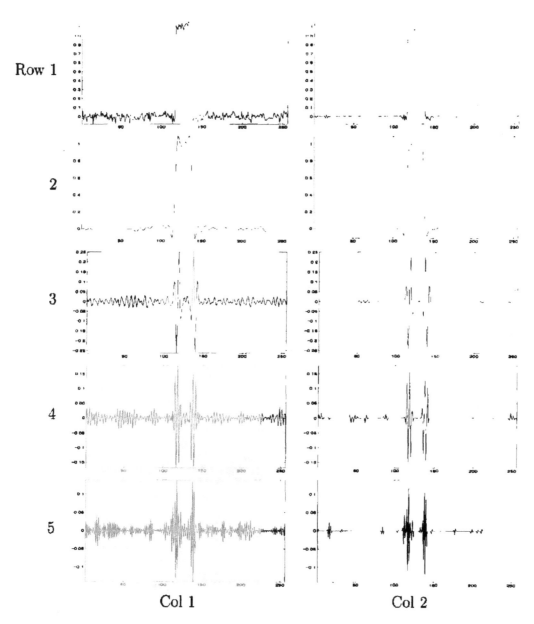

Figure 4.3: An Example of Overcomplete Wavelet Denoising.

Where:

Col 1: An perfect impulse contaminated by white Gaussian noise (row1) and its level 2 overcomplete wavelet packet representation (row2-5);

Col 2: Overcomplete wavelet packet representation after shrinking operations (row2-5) and reconstructed signal (row1).

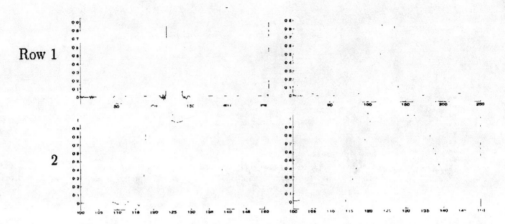

Figure 4.4: Comparison of Overcomplete Wavelet Shrinkage Denoising with Linear Smoothing Using the Signal of (row 1,col 1) of Figure 4.3.
Where:

Row 1: Overcomplete wavelet shrinkage (left, the same as row 1, col 2 of Figure 4.3) and linear smoothing (right);

Row 2: Local zoom-in with overlay of the original noisy signal.

average normalized power in a period T is thus

$$\overline{W} = \frac{1}{T} \int_0^T i^2(t)dt = \frac{1}{2}A^2.$$

Therefore, the average normalized power of a harmonic signal is proportional to its *amplitude* squared.

For an arbitrary waveform $i(t)$, one can decompose it into harmonic components using Fourier analysis:

$$i(t) = \int_{-\infty}^{\infty} I(\omega)e^{j2\pi ft}df.$$

By the same token, energy density (per unit time and per unit frequency) at frequency ω is proportional to the amplitude squared of the component $I(\omega)e^{j2\pi ft}$, which is $|I(\omega)|^2$. The function $|I(\omega)|^2$ describes power distribution in the frequency domain and is called *power density spectrum* [49, page 66].

The above concepts can be extended to overcomplete wavelet representations, by extending the concept of amplitude to "envelope" [26, chapter 4], or "local amplitude." An overcomplete wavelet representation is consist of bandpass components.

Since any bandpass waveform may be represented by $A(t) \sin(\omega_c t + \alpha(t))$ [26, page 229], where $A(t)$ is the envelope and ω_c is the associated carrier frequency, an overcomplete wavelet representation $\{w_k(t)|_{0 \le k \le M-1}\}$ may be rewritten in the form of:

$$\{A(\omega_k, t) \sin(\omega_k t + \alpha_k(t))|_{0 \le k \le M-1}\}.$$

Thus, squared envelopes $\{A^2(\omega_k, t)\}$ shall describe the power density distribution of the overcomplete wavelet representation in the time-frequency plane (also called "phase space" in [12]). Figure 4.5 shows examples of such a distribution.

For time-frequency representations using complex Gabor filters [6], envelopes may be extracted by simply performing a modulus operation on two quadratic components. However, for representations with real analyzing filters, such as overcomplete wavelet representations, more sophisticated envelope detection algorithms are needed. We present the next two envelope detection algorithms and investigate their performance.

4.4.1 Envelope Detection by Hilbert Transform

The envelope of a narrowband bandpass signal can be computed by a corresponding analytical signal [51]. For a signal $x(t)$, the analytic signal is defined by:

$$\tilde{x}(t) = x(t) + j\hat{x}(t),$$

where $\hat{x}(t)$ is the Hilbert transform of $x(t)$,

$$\hat{x}(t) = \frac{1}{\pi} \int_{-\infty}^{\infty} \frac{x(\eta)}{t - \eta} d\eta.$$

The envelope of the original signal $x(t)$ is then simply the modulus of the analytic signal $\tilde{x}(t)$:

$$e(t) = |\tilde{x}(t)| = \sqrt{x^2(t) + \hat{x}^2(t)} .$$

The frequency characteristics of the Hilbert transform can be expressed by:

$$H(\omega) = \begin{cases} -j & , \quad \omega >= 0 \\ j & , \quad otherwise. \end{cases}$$

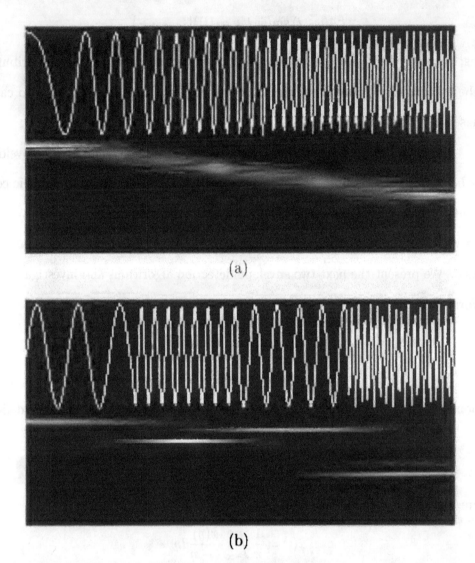

(a)

(b)

Figure 4.5: Two Examples of Power Density Distribution of Overcomplete Wavelet Packet Representations.

Legend:

(a) A linear chirp signal, the same as in Figure 3.4(b);

(b) A multi-segment pure tone signal with frequencies $\omega_0 = 0.08\pi$, $\omega_1 = 0.25\pi$, $\omega_2 = 0.15\pi$ and $\omega_3 = 0.55\pi$, in the order of occurrence. The overcomplete wavelet representation and visual arrangements are the same as in Figure 3.4.

49

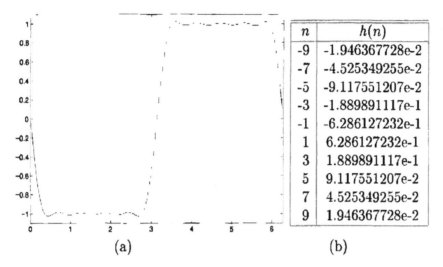

n	$h(n)$
-9	-1.946367728e-2
-7	-4.525349255e-2
-5	-9.117551207e-2
-3	-1.889891117e-1
-1	-6.286127232e-1
1	6.286127232e-1
3	1.889891117e-1
5	9.117551207e-2
7	4.525349255e-2
9	1.946367728e-2

(a)   (b)

Figure 4.6: A FIR Hilbert Transformer.

Legend:

(a) the imaginary part of the frequency response (the real part is zero).

(b) nonzero coefficients.

Therefore, the Fourier transform of the analytical signal $\tilde{x}(t)$ is:

$$\widetilde{X}(\omega) = \begin{cases} 2X(\omega) & , \quad \omega >= 0 \\ 0 & , \quad otherwise. \end{cases}$$

For implementations in discrete-time domain, approximate FIR Hilbert transformers may be designed by windowing the ideal frequency response [49]. Figure 4.6 shows an example. It is a type–III FIR Hilbert transformer designed with parameters $M = 18$, and $\beta = 2.629$ [49, page 680]. This Hilbert transformer is antisymmetric, of length 19 and has only 10 nonzero coefficients.

4.4.2 Envelope Detection by Zero Crossings

In this method, the maximum absolute value between two adjacent zero-crossings is first found, and then assigned to each point within the interval.

Algorithm 4.4.1 (Envelope by Zero Crossings) *For a given array $x(1 : N)$, start from the index $i = 1$, find the next index k which is either a zero crossing point or a zero valued point $x(k) = 0$ or the other end point $k = N$, whoever is first encountered, assign the maximum absolute value $A_{i,k} = \max\{|x(n)|_{i \le n \le k}\}$ to all the elements*

$\{x(n)|_{i \le n \le k}\}$. *Advance the index $i = k$ and repeat the process until reaching the other end.*

4.4.3 Comparison Between the Two Detectors

We compared two envelope detectors by their working frequency range and robustness under noise perturbations. For pure-tone impulse signals, both did well in the middle range ($\omega \in [0.1\pi, 0.7\pi]$). While Hilbert transform was unacceptable at the low end ($\omega < 0.1\pi$), the zero-crossing approach did poor at the high end ($\omega > 0.7\pi$). The test cases were shown in the rows 1 and 2 of Figure 4.7. We constructed a noisy impulse by introducing a random frequency perturbation:

$$s(n) = \sin((\omega_0 + 0.05 * RANDN(n))n),$$

where $RANDN$ (a MATLAB function) is a random noise with normal distribution, and filtered it with a Lemarié filter $H_1(\omega)$. This case was included in the row 3 of Figure 4.7. We found that the zero-crossing method exhibited edge-preserving smoothing characteristics and was more robust to wide-band noise.

4.4.4 Comparison with Other Energy Operators

A useful and simple energy operator was analyzed on [46]. The operator Ψ for a discrete signal $x(n)$ was given as

$$\Psi[x(n)] = x^2(n) - x(n+1)x(n-1).$$

However, this operator differs with envelope detectors in the way that its value on a pure tone signal is not only proportional to the amplitude squared but also a function of frequency [46]:

$$\Psi[A\sin(\omega_0 n + \alpha)] = A^2 \sin^2(\omega_0).$$

4.4.5 Two Dimensional Envelope Detection

Next we extended the 1D envelope detection algorithms for the analysis of two-dimensional image signals. In the frequency domain, a two-dimensional analytic

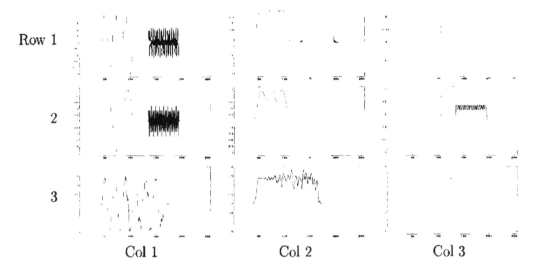

Figure 4.7: Comparison of the Two Envelope Detectors.

Where:

Col 1: Input signals (top row, $\omega_0 = 0.1\pi$, $\omega_1 = 0.5\pi$; center row, $\omega_0 = 0.05\pi$, $\omega_1 = 0.75\pi$; bottom row, noisy signal with $\omega_0 = 0.1\pi$).

Col 2: Envelopes detected via the 19-tap Hilbert transformer.

Col 3: Envelopes detected via the zero-crossing method.

signal may be obtained by setting an appropriate half plane to zero, based on its orientation. That is, for a 2D signal $f(x, y)$, the Fourier transform of an analytic signal $\tilde{f}(x, y)$ is either:

$$\tilde{F}(\omega_x, \omega_y) = \begin{cases} 2F(\omega_x, \omega_y) & , \quad \omega_x >= 0 \\ 0 & , \quad otherwise \end{cases}$$

or,

$$\tilde{F}(\omega_x, \omega_y) = \begin{cases} 2F(\omega_x, \omega_y) & , \quad \omega_y >= 0 \\ 0 & , \quad otherwise. \end{cases}$$

For the 2D filters constructed by the tensor product method with halfband filters, the equivalent complex quadrature filters exhibited the frequency response shown in Figure 4.8. Notice that lowpass and diagonal components may have an alternate arrangement by zeroing out the left or bottom half plane.

This separable property allowed one to compute the envelope of a 2D signal using the 1D algorithms described earlier in a straightforward manner, described in the following.

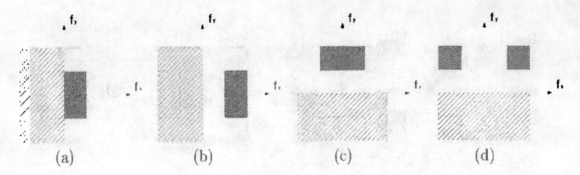

Figure 4.8: Frequency Response of Equivalent Complex Quadrature Filters (level 1).
Legend:

    (a) lowpass channel

    (b) vertical channel

    (c) horizontal channel

    (d) diagonal channel

The diagonal shadowed areas identify zeroed half planes.

Algorithm 4.4.2 (2D Envelope Detection) *For a given 2D array $w(m,n)$ and its orientation. If its orientation is horizontal, apply the 1D envelope detector column-wise; If its orientation is vertical, apply the 1D envelope detector row-wise; Otherwise, apply the 1D envelope detector column-wise.*

CHAPTER 5
APPLICATION I: TEXTURE SEGMENTATION

5.1 Introduction

In this chapter, we shall apply overcomplete wavelet representations to the problem of segmentation of textured images.

However, it seems that we were back to the beginning. It may sound odd, but it is true that there is not even a precise definition of "texture," let alone "texture segmentation" [61]. In spite of the difficulty, there is a general consensus that texture is a property of area. We felt that the concept of texture is parallel to the concept of "local frequency" for an non-stationary signal. The concept of local frequency is easy to understand. It describes the rate of change occurs in a window around a particular time. Yet there is not a unique definition of local frequency. Therefore, our treatment of texture segmentation is to embrace it into the paradigm of time-frequency analysis.

There have been many research works on texture segmentation using the concept of spatial-frequency representation. The analyzing functions used by researchers include:

- Laws microtexture masks (filters) [24]
- Complex prolate spheroidal sequences [64]
- Complex Gabor functions [6, 19]
- Real Gabor functions [30]
- The Wigner distribution [54]

More recently, wavelet and wavelet packet representations have been added to the list [34, 35, 36, 62, 9, 37].

A segmentation process usually consists of two distinct phases: feature extraction and clustering. Features for texture representation are of crucial importance

53

for accomplishing segmentation [27]. In this chapter, we demonstrated that over-complete wavelet packet representation and envelope detection make a good feature extraction scheme on a variety of both natural and synthetic textured images.

5.2 Texture Feature Extraction

The texture features we chose are the envelopes of overcomplete wavelet representations. The interpretation of the feature is that their squares corresponds to spatial-frequency power density distribution as pointed out in the last chapter. The feature extraction thus consists of two stages: 1) overcomplete wavelet packet decomposition and 2) envelope detection.

For 2D envelope detection on overcomplete wavelet packet representations, we classified each node in the decomposition tree into four possible categories, taking into account orientation, as follows:

- The root node is *omnidirectional*.

- The node last filtered by $G_l(\omega_x)H_l(\omega_y)$ corresponds to *vertical-orientation*. (Highpass filter G_l is applied row-wise and lowpass filter H_l column-wise.)

- The node last filtered by $H_l(\omega_x)G_l(\omega_y)$ corresponds to *horizontal-orientation*. (Lowpass filter H_l is applied row-wise and highpass filter G_l column-wise.)

- The node last filtered by $G_l(\omega_x)G_l(\omega_y)$ corresponds to *diagonal-orientation*. (Highpass filter G_l is applied row-wise and highpass filter G_l column-wise)

- The node last filtered by $H_l(\omega_x)H_l(\omega_y)$ has the same orientation as its parent. (Lowpass filter H_l is applied row-wise and lowpass filter H_l column-wise)

At the end of feature extraction, each sample of a signal was attached a feature vector. In our case, such a feature vector is consist of envelopes of overcomplete wavelet packet representation. It is possible to apply a *monotonic* function to the feature space to transform it into another feature space. For example, a square function x^2 will transform the envelope space into a space of power density distribution and log function $\log(x)$ will transform the envelope space into a space of log spectral.

5.3 Considerations on Filter Selection

We raised the issue of filter selection in the Chapter 3 on overcomplete wavelet representations. For the application of segmentation, we argued that symmetry, frequency response, and boundary accuracy are important factors in the selection of filters for feature extraction. In the following, we discuss these constraints in terms of overall performance.

- **Symmetry.** For accomplishing texture segmentation, accuracy in texture boundary detection is crucial for reliable performance. In this application, filters with symmetry or antisymmetry are clearly favored. Such filters have a linear phase response, where the delay (shift) is predictable. Alternatively, filters with nonlinear phase may introduce complex distortion. Moreover, symmetric or anti-symmetric filters are also advantageous in alleviating boundary effects through simple methods of mirror extension (see Appendix D).

- **Optimal Frequency Response.** In order to derive an ideal filter frequency response for the chosen feature, we considered a two-band filter bank with input signals of infinite length consisting of two segments with distinct pure tones. The input signals can be written as:

$$s(n) = \begin{cases} A_1 \cos(\omega_1 n + \alpha_1) & ,n < 0, \\ A_2 \cos(\omega_2 n + \alpha_2) & ,n \geq 0, \end{cases}$$

where $A_1 > 0$ and $A_2 > 0$. Except for the boundary ($n=0$), we derived the feature vectors (envelopes of channel outputs) as,

$$\vec{T} = (e_H, e_G) = \begin{cases} \vec{T}_{left} = (A_1 |H(\omega_1)|, A_1 |G(\omega_1)|) & ,n < 0, \\ \vec{T}_{right} = (A_2 |H(\omega_2)|, A_2 |G(\omega_2)|) & ,n \geq 0. \end{cases}$$

The angle θ between vectors $\vec{T}_{left}$ and $\vec{T}_{right}$ is

$$\cos^{-1} \left(\frac{|H(\omega_1)H(\omega_2)| + |G(\omega_1)G(\omega_2)|}{\sqrt{|H(\omega_1)|^2 + |G(\omega_1)|^2}\sqrt{|H(\omega_2)|^2 + |G(\omega_2)|^2}} \right),$$

and is bound by $0 \leq \theta \leq \frac{\pi}{2}$. The distance between the two classes in the feature space is then

$$D = \sqrt{\left|\vec{T}_{left}\right|^2 + \left|\vec{T}_{right}\right|^2 - 2\left|\vec{T}_{left}\right|\left|\vec{T}_{right}\right|\cos(\theta)} .$$

For $\theta = \frac{\pi}{2}$, vectors $\vec{T}_{left}$ and $\vec{T}_{right}$ are orthogonal, and the distance D reaches its maximum. Clearly, the maximum distance in feature space between any two classes is optimal for segmentation and classification applications, in the sense that the classes are better seperated and more robust to noise perturbations. Notice that for $H(\omega_1) \neq 0$ and $G(\omega_2) \neq 0$, $\cos(\theta) = 0$ if and only if $G(\omega_1) = 0$ and $H(\omega_2) = 0$. This means that optimal filter banks should have no overlap in the frequency domain, and thus filter $H(\omega)$ with optimal frequency response must be a perfect half-band filter. Indeed, [50] derived a similar optimal filter for image coding applications.

Of course such ideal filters cannot be realized in practice. Based on the preceding discussion, filter bands overlapping in the frequency domain tend to *reduce* class distance in feature space. Therefore, a filter $H(\omega)$ with a large stop-band attenuation and flat pass-band frequency response is desirable.

- **Spatial Localization.** There are two types of boundaries for signals of finite length: 1) boundaries of regions exhibiting distinct characteristics, and 2) the physical boundaries of a data segment. Feature vectors close to the boundaries will be affected. The size of the affected region depends on the length of the channel filters, and the distribution of filter coefficients. Therefore, filters of short length and fast decay shall be better suited for boundary detection.

Unfortunately, the preceding three criteria cannot be satisfied simultaneously. As previously pointed out, quadrature mirror filters (QMF) with compact support cannot be symmetric or anti-symmetric. This means that a symmetric constraint on any QMF will be in conflict with spatial localization goals. Moreover, large attenuation in the stop band requires a longer filter, which in turn degrades the filter's spatial localization. Again, we faced the limitation of the uncertainty principle, and the previous discussions about the uncertainty factor of a filter bank is applicable here.

In this study, we chose the Lemarié filters for its symmetry and good frequency characteristics.

5.4   The Basic Isodata Clustering Algorithm

Segmentation algorithms accept a set of features as input and output a consistent labeling for each pixel. Basically, this is a multi-dimensional data clustering problem with no general algorithm available [23]. Clustering algorithms that have been previously used for texture segmentation can be divided into two categories: 1) *supervised segmentation* and 2) *unsupervised segmentation*.

In practice, unsupervised segmentation is often desirable and easy to validate. It is particularly useful in those cases where testing samples are difficult to prepare (making supervised segmentation infeasible). Thus, we used a *Baisc Isodata* clustering algorithm [18, page 201].

Algorithm 5.4.1 (Basic Isodata) *Given a 2D image array x of structure containing feature vectors and label fields, and the number of classes N_c,*

   Step 1. *Scan the representation matrix x in raster order. For every pixel encountered, randomly pick a label from set $\{0, ..., N_c-1\}$ and assign it to the pixel.*

   Step 2. *Compute the class center $\{\vec{C}_k \mid_{0 \leq k \leq N_c-1}\}$ by calculating the mean vector for each class k.*

Step 3. *Rescan the whole representation matrix x, and assign pixel (i, j) to the class k if the Euclidean distance between the feature vector of the pixel and the class center $\vec{C}_k$ is the closest.*

Step 4. *If no pixel changes its class in the* **Step 3**, *stop; else, go to the* **Step 2**.

This algorithm differs from a K-means algorithm [29] in only one aspect: Basic Isodata updates class centers after a complete scan of an input feature set while K-means updates for every reassignment. In our experiments, Basic Isodata outperformed K-means for almost all cases.

5.5 Postprocessing

The Basic Isodata algorithm labels each pixel independently and does not take into account the high correlation between neighboring pixels. A postprocessing stage, such as the relaxation labeling [25], can be used to incorporate some neighborhood constraint into the segmentation process.

For simplicity, we used median filtering as our postprocessing to simulate the benefit of a local constraint. In particular, a 5×5 median filtering was repeatedly applied to an initial segmentation until no change of labeling occurred.

5.6 Experimental Results

Our segmentation algorithm was tested on both one-dimensional signals and two-dimensional textured images. Our test images included samples of two distinct families of textures. In all examples shown, straightforward envelopes of the overcomplete wavelet packet representation were used as texture feature.

5.6.1 One-dimensional Signals

Figure 5.1 shows the segmentation of a signal consist of a sinusoid segment and a triangular segment with the same period (sixteen samples) and amplitude.

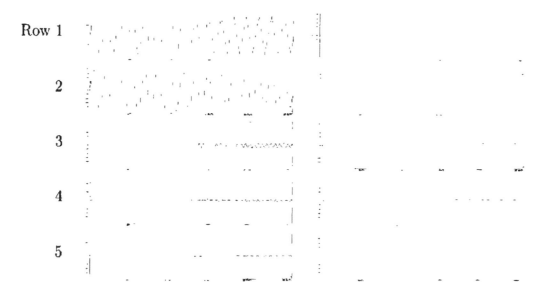

Row 1

2

3

4

5

Figure 5.1: Segmentation of a 1D Signal Consists of Triangular Waveform and Sinusoid.
   Where:
   Row 1: the original signal and the segmentation result;
   Row 2-5: the overcomplete wavelet packet representation and envelopes.

With envelopes of four channels of the Level 2 representation, the perfect result was achieved. Figure 5.2 is a segmentation example of a noisy signal consist of two sinusoid segments ($\omega=0.3\pi$ and $\omega=0.5\pi$) contaminated by white Gaussian noise. Envelopes of eight channels of the Level 3 representation was able to achieve the perfect result.

5.6.2 Natural Textures

Here we used textures obtained from the Brodatz album [7] and public archive. Each testing sample was first histogram-equalized so that a segmentation result based only on first order statistics was not possible. Experimental results are displayed in Figure 5.3. Experimentally, we observed that a lower order Lemarié-Battle filter ($p=1$) performed well in boundary detection (Figure 5.3 (b)), while the higher order Lemarié-Battle filter ($p=2$) did a better job within non-boundary (internal) regions.

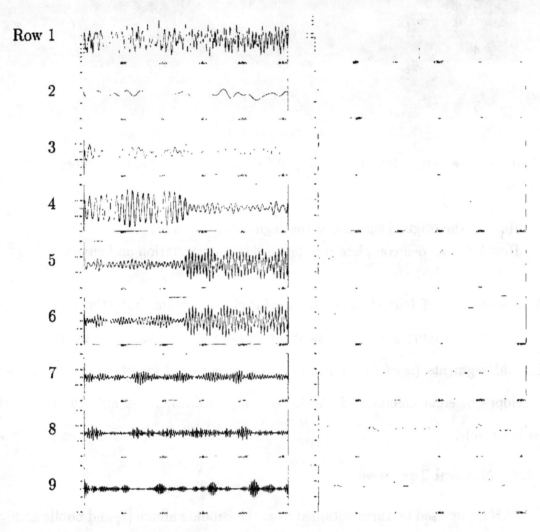

Figure 5.2: Segmentation of a Noisy 1D Signal Consists of Two Pure Tone Segments. Where:

Row 1: the original signal and the segmentation result,

Row 2-9: the overcomplete wavelet packet representation and envelopes.

Row 1

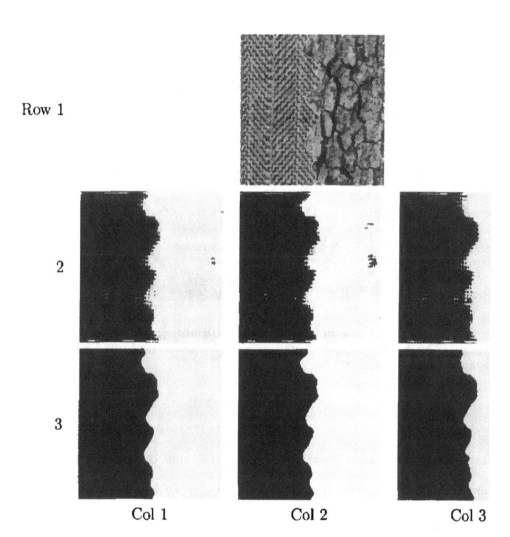

2

3

Col 1   Col 2   Col 3

Figure 5.3: Segmentation Results of a Image Consist of Natural Textures. Where:

Row 1: Test image T1 (256×256, 8-bit) consists of D17, herringborn weave and bark (true boundary overlaid for display only).

Row 2: Clustering results using features extracted from a Level 4 filter bank generated by (Col 1) Lemarié-Battle filter of $p = 1$, (Col 2) autocorrelation function of Lemarié-Battle filter of $p=1$, (Col 3) Lemarié-Battle filter of $p=2$. The zero-crossing algorithm were used for envelope detection.

Row 3: Final segmentations after postprocessing.

5.6.3 Synthetic Textures

We tested the performance of our algorithm on several texture images synthesized from random noise based on [27].

- **Gaussian Lowpass and Bandpass Textures**. The images were generated by filtering a white Gaussian noise with mean of zero and standard deviation of 30 with a Gaussian filter of frequency response (in polar coordinate):

$$G(r,\theta) = e^{-(\theta-\theta_0)^2/(2\pi^2 B_0^2)} e^{-(r-F_c)^2/(2S_r^2)} .$$

- **Filtered Impulse Noise (FIN)**. The images were generated by filtering a random impulse image $I(m,n)$ generated by:

$$I(m,n) = \begin{cases} 1.0, & if\ RAN \geq T, \\ 0.0, & if\ RAN < T, \end{cases}$$

where $RAN \in (0.0, 1.0)$ is a random number with uniform distribution, with Gaussian impulse response:

$$g(m,n) = e^{-m^2/(2S_x^2)} e^{-n^2/(2S_y^2)}.$$

In both cases, images were linearly-scaled into the range of $[0, 255]$.

Figure 5.4 shows a segmentation result on a Gaussian lowpass texture image, and Figure 5.5 shows a segmentation result on a filtered impulse noise (FIN) texture image. For this difficult test image $T3$, the algorithm achieved outstanding performance.

We also tested our algorithm on a texture image containing regular and sparse elements. Figure 5.6 demonstrates the accurate segmentation result.

5.7 Summary and Discussion

A quantitative comparison, presenting the accuracy of our segmentation results of textured images is summarized in Table 5.1. This performance is consistent

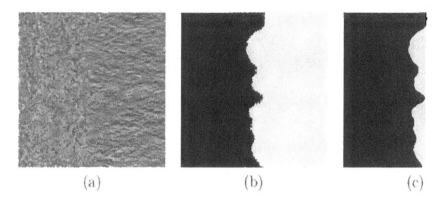

Figure 5.4: Segmentation of a Synthetic Gaussian Lowpassed Texture Image.
Legend:

(a) Test image T2 (256×256, 8-bit): Gaussian LP, left: isotropic $F_c = 0$, $S_r = 60$; right: non-isotropic $F_c = 0$, $S_r = 60$, $\theta_0 = 0$, $B_0 = 0.175$.

(b) Initial segmentation (Lemarié-Battle filter of $p = 1$, Level 4 and zero-crossing envelope detection)

(c) Final segmentation after postprocessing.

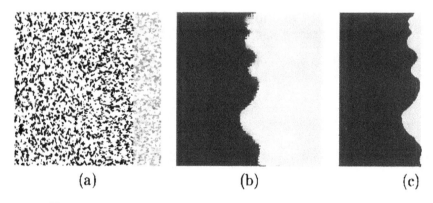

Figure 5.5: Segmentation of a Synthetic FIN Texture Image.
Legend:

(a) Test image T3 (256×256, 8-bit): Filtered impulse noise, left: non-isotropic $T = 0.15$, $S_x = 1.0$, $S_y = 1.5$; right: non-isotropic $T = 0.15$, $S_x = 2.0$, $S_y = 1.0$.

(b) Initial segmentation (Lemarié-Battle filter of $p = 1$, Level 4 and zero-crossing envelope detection)

(c) Final segmentation after postprocessing.

(a) (b) (c)

Figure 5.6: Segmentation of a Synthetic Texture Image with Line Patterns.
Legend:

(a) Test image T4 (256×256, 8-bit)

(b) Final segmentation (Lemarié-Battle filter of $p = 1$, Level 3 and zero-crossing based envelope detection).

(c) Detected boundary overlaid with the original image.

Table 5.1: Boundary Accuracy of the Segmentation Results.

Test image	Maximum ABE	Average ABE	$\pm\sigma$
T1	11.0	3.2	2.6
T2	15.0	2.9	2.4
T3	11.0	2.9	2.6

ABE: Absolute Boundary Error (in pixels).

with the difficulty of segmentation perceived by human observers. We observed that boundary errors are dependent on shape *i.e.*, complex boundaries yielded higher variance.

Overcomplete wavelet packet representations and envelope features provide a versatile and flexible framework. The examples showed that satisfactory results can be achieved. Based on our experiments, low-order Lemarié filter ($p = 1$) achieved the best results. However, we are aware that there were several important parameters to be determined manually for the segmentation algorithm to work. These include the configuration of the representation and the number of classes. On the face of lacking a precise definition of the problem, we believed that no mathematical solution is possible, and these parameters can only be designed case-by-case for particular applications.

Comparing with Gabor filters, overcomplete wavelet packet representations possess several potential advantages for further exploration:

- channel filters cover *exactly* the frequency domain (provide a mathematically complete representation) without significant overlap, thus greatly reducing correlations between features extracted from distinct channels

- adaptive pruning of a decomposition tree makes possible the reduction of computational complexity and the length of feature vectors

- by moving up the decomposition tree, feature vectors at distinct resolution levels can be obtained to increase the accuracy of boundary detection

CHAPTER 6
APPLICATION II: IMAGE DEBLURRING

6.1 Introduction

Image deblurring is a special case of signal restoration. The goal is to recover an image which is blurred and usually degraded by noise. During the past two decades, large amount of research works have been done in this area [33, 2, 28].

Unlike the texture segmentation, image deblurring is a well defined problem. The mathematical model commonly used to describe the degradation process is a convolution and an additive noise, written as:

$$y(k_1, k_2) = d(k_1, k_2) * x(k_1, k_2) + n(k_1, k_2),$$

where $x(k_1, k_2)$ is the original image, $y(k_1, k_2)$ is the observed image, $d(k_1, k_2)$ is the impulse response of the blurring operator, $n(k_1, k_2)$ is the noise and the symbol $*$ stands for convolution. The deblurring problem is to restore the original image $x(k_1, k_2)$ from the degraded image $y(k_1, k_2)$. This is thus a *linear inverse* problem.

At the first glance, the problem seems solvable. Assuming known impulse response of the blurring process and the absent of noise, one may formally derive the solution in the frequency domain as:

$$X(\omega_1, \omega_2) = Y(\omega_1, \omega_2)/D(\omega_1, \omega_2).$$

This is the simplest, most intuitive approach and is called *inverse filtering* [2, 28, 22]. However, the frequency response $D(\omega_1, \omega_2)$ associated with a blurring process usually has zeros in the frequency plane and its reciprocal is thus *unbounded*. In the other point of view, blurring generally causes irreversible information loss even without the existence of noise. By taking into account of noise, the inverse filtering approach

66

would produce a restoration:

$$X'(\omega_1, \omega_2) = Y(\omega_1, \omega_2)/D(\omega_1, \omega_2) = X(\omega_1, \omega_2) + N(\omega_1, \omega_2)/D(\omega_1, \omega_2).$$

In this case, the closeness of the restored image X' to the original image X is hinged on the strength of the noise N. Notice that the precise waveform of the noise is unknown and thus cannot be completely subtracted from the observed image Y.

Inverse problems associated with a unbounded inverse operator is said to be *ill-posed* [33. 14]. The traditional mathematical tool for dealing with such problems is *regularization methods* [60].

In this chapter, we shall apply overcomplete wavelet packet representations to the deblurring problem. Our approach explicitly suppresses noise using the nonlinear shrink operator and approximates an inverse filter using the gain operator.

6.2 Review of Some Deblurring Techniques

In this section, we shall review modified inverse filters, Wiener filters and the more recent theory of wavelet-vaguelette inversion.

6.2.1 Modified Inverse Filters

For blurs having zeros in the frequency plane, there are two modifications available to make a bounded inverse filter.

1. **Gain-limited Inverse Filter.** The idea is simply setting a upper-bound for the magnitude of frequency response to grow, as described below:

$$F(\omega_x, \omega_y) = \begin{cases} 1/R & , \quad 0 < D(\omega_x, \omega_y) < R, \\ 1/D(\omega_x, \omega_y) & , \quad |D(\omega_x, \omega_y)| > R, \\ -1/R & , \quad -R < D(\omega_x, \omega_y) < 0, \end{cases} \tag{6.1}$$

   where R is a positive real value and $D(\omega_x, \omega_y)$ is a real filter.

2. **Pseudo-inverse Filter**[28, page 276]. This is the same as the gain-limited inverse filter except the constant gain region set to zero:

$$F(\omega_x, \omega_y) = \begin{cases} 0 & , \quad |D(\omega_x, \omega_y)| \leq R, \\ 1/D(\omega_x, \omega_y) & , \quad |D(\omega_x, \omega_y)| > R, \end{cases} \tag{6.2}$$

where R is a positive real value.

Both approaches have their pros and cons. The advantage of the gain-limited inverse filter is that it is continuous in the frequency domain. The disadvantage is that the passband of $|D(\omega_x, \omega_y)| < R$ may significantly enhance wideband noise. In opposite, the pseudo-inverse filter will completely wipe out anything outside its region of inversion by sacrificing the continuity.

6.2.2 Wiener Filters

The idea of the Wiener filter is to choose a deblurring filter f to minimize the mean square restoration error defined as [18, 2, 22]:

$$\mathcal{E} = E\left\{[x'(k_1, k_2) - x(k_1, k_2)]^2\right\},$$

where $x' = f * (d * x + n)$ and E denotes mathematical expectation [49]. Assume that noise n is a random field with zero mean and is independent of x, the expression of $\mathcal{E}$ can be evaluated as:

$$
\begin{aligned}
\mathcal{E} &= E\left[(f*d*x - x)^2 - 2(f*d*x - x)(f*n) + (f*n)^2\right] \\
&= E\left[((f*d - \delta)*x)^2\right] + E\left[(f*n)^2\right] \\
&= \frac{1}{4\pi^2}\int_{-\pi}^{\pi}\int_{-\pi}^{\pi}\left[|FD - 1|^2\Phi_{xx} + |F|^2\Phi_{nn}\right]d\omega_1 d\omega_2,
\end{aligned}
$$

where F, D, Φ_{xx} and Φ_{nn} are all functions of (ω_1, ω_2), and Φ_{xx} and Φ_{nn} are the *power density spectrum* of the signal and noise [49, Section 2.10], respectively. Furthermore, the integrand can be factored as:

$$
\begin{aligned}
&|FD - 1|^2\Phi_{xx} + |F|^2\Phi_{nn} \\
&= (F - 1/D)(F^* - 1/D^*)|D|^2\Phi_{xx} + FF^*\Phi_{nn} \\
&= (FF^* - F/D^* - F^*/D + 1/|D|^2)|D|^2\Phi_{xx} + FF^*\Phi_{nn} \\
&= FF^*\left(|D|^2\Phi_{xx} + \Phi_{nn}\right) - (F/D^* + F^*/D)|D|^2\Phi_{xx} + \Phi_{xx} \\
&= \left[FF^* - (F/D^* + F^*/D)\frac{|D|^2\Phi_{xx}}{|D|^2\Phi_{xx}+\Phi_{nn}}\right]\left(|D|^2\Phi_{xx} + \Phi_{nn}\right) + \Phi_{xx} \\
&= \left[\left|F - \frac{D^*\Phi_{xx}}{|D|^2\Phi_{xx}+\Phi_{nn}}\right|^2 - \left(\frac{|D|\Phi_{xx}}{|D|^2\Phi_{xx}+\Phi_{nn}}\right)^2\right]\left(|D|^2\Phi_{xx} + \Phi_{nn}\right) + \Phi_{xx} \\
&= \left|F - \frac{D^*\Phi_{xx}}{|D|^2\Phi_{xx}+\Phi_{nn}}\right|^2\left(|D|^2\Phi_{xx} + \Phi_{nn}\right) - \frac{|D|^2\Phi_{xx}^2}{|D|^2\Phi_{xx}+\Phi_{nn}} + \Phi_{xx}.
\end{aligned}
$$

Since the first term is large than or equal to zero, the optimal deblurring filter (Wiener filter) is thus

$$F(\omega_1, \omega_2) = \frac{D^*(\omega_1, \omega_2)\Phi_{xx}(\omega_1, \omega_2)}{|D(\omega_1, \omega_2)|^2 \Phi_{xx}(\omega_1, \omega_2) + \Phi_{nn}(\omega_1, \omega_2)}, \tag{6.3}$$

which can be rewritten in terms of the signal-to-noise power ratio

$$F(\omega_1, \omega_2) = \frac{D^*(\omega_1, \omega_2)}{|D(\omega_1, \omega_2)|^2 + \Phi_{nn}(\omega_1, \omega_2)/\Phi_{xx}(\omega_1, \omega_2)} .$$

For white Gaussian noise, $\Phi_{nn}(\omega_1, \omega_2) = N_0$. The power spectrum $\Phi_{xx}(\omega_1, \omega_2)$ characterizes correlation property of the signal x. As the correlation usually falls off as the sample distant increases, $\Phi_{xx}(\omega_1, \omega_2)$ usually is a lowpass function. If the signal has no correlation among its adjacent samples, $\Phi_{xx}(\omega_1, \omega_2) = S_0$, and the signal-to-noise power ratio equals to a constant $S_0/N_0 = 1/R$. In this case, the Wiener filter is reduced to

$$F(\omega_1, \omega_2) = \frac{D^*(\omega_1, \omega_2)}{|D(\omega_1, \omega_2)|^2 + R} . \tag{6.4}$$

Comparing with the gain-limited inverse filter and the pseudo-inverse filter, the Wiener filter of (6.4) possesses both merits of continuity and noise suppression.

6.2.3 Wavelet-Vaguelette Inversion

The combination of wavelet-vaguelette decomposition (WVD) and nonlinear shrinkage of WVD coefficients was proposed by Donoho [14] for linear inversion problems involving dilation-homogeneous operators. An operator Γ with such property is commutable with a dilation operator D_a such that

$$\Gamma D_a = a^\alpha D_a \Gamma ,$$

where α is a constant, and D_a is the dilation operator defined as

$$D_a[f(t)] = f(at) .$$

The WVD involves three sets of functions: an orthogonal wavelet basis $\{\psi_{j,k}(t) = 2^{j/2}\psi(2^j t - k)\}$ and two near-orthogonal sets $\{u_{j,k}(t) = 2^{j/2}u(2^j t - k)\}$ and

$\{v_{j,k}(t) = 2^{j/2}v(2^j t - k)\}$. The three sets are related by the quasi-singular value relations

$$\Gamma\psi_{j,k} = \gamma_j v_{j,k}, \tag{6.5}$$

$$\Gamma^* u_{j,k} = \gamma_j \psi_{j,k}, \tag{6.6}$$

where quasi-singular values γ_j depend on resolution index j but not spatial index k. Moreover, the two sets $\{u_{j,k}(t)\}$ and $\{v_{j,k}(t)\}$ satisfy biothogonality

$$\int_{-\infty}^{\infty} u_{j,k}(t)v_{m,n}^*(t)dt = \delta_{j,m}\delta_{k,n},$$

and near-orthogonality

$$\int_{-\infty}^{\infty}\left(\sum_{j,k} a_{j,k}u_{j,k}(t)\right)^2 dt \asymp \sum_{j,k} a_{j,k}^2,$$
$$\int_{-\infty}^{\infty}\left(\sum_{j,k} a_{j,k}v_{j,k}(t)\right)^2 dt \asymp \sum_{j,k} a_{j,k}^2.$$

Linking everything together, the reproducing formula of the WVD is expressed by

$$x(t) = \sum_{j,k}\left[\Gamma x, u_{j,k}\right]\gamma_j^{-1}\psi_{j,k}(t),$$

where $[x,y] = \int_{-\infty}^{\infty} x(t)y^*(t)dt$ is the inner product of x and y.

Finally, the WVD inversion of a white Gaussian contaminated measurement $y(t) = \Gamma x(t) + n(t)$ may be achieved via

$$x'(t) = \sum_{j,k}\mathcal{K}_{t_j}\left\{[y, u_{j,k}]\gamma_j^{-1}\right\}\psi_{j,k}(t), \tag{6.7}$$

where $\mathcal{K}_{t_j}$ is the nonlinear shrinking operator defined by (4.4). Notice that the threshold t_j depends only on resolution j.

6.2.4 Discussion

The Wiener filter provided a powerful tool for linear inversion problems. Given the statistics of both image and noise processes, one can design a optimal filter. However, Wiener filter belongs to the *linear* filtering paradigm and works in the frequency domain. The linear property determines that it has to trade-off between smoothing out noise and sharpening up edges.

In the opposite, the wavelet-vaguelette approach deployed *nonlinear* shrinkage to combat noise in the time domain. It is characterized by three components: 1) dyadic analyzing and synthesizing functions determined by the blurring operator Γ; 2) level-dependent gain factors γ_j^{-1}; and 3) nonlinear shrinkage with level-dependent thresholds t_j. The nonlinearity enables it to achieve better compromise between denoising and sharpening. However, it is limited to dilation-homogeneous operators only, excluding the most commonly encountered Gaussian and uniform blurs [14]. Moreover, the theory was developed in the continuous-time domain.

The limitation of the WVD inversion lies on its insistence of the quasi-singular value relations (Eqs. (6.5) and (6.6)). For a convolution operator Γ with kernel $h(t)$, in the frequency domain (6.5) is equal to

$$H(\omega)\Psi(2^{-j}\omega) = \gamma_j V(2^{-j}\omega). \tag{6.8}$$

Let $\omega' = 2^k\omega$ and plug it into (6.8), we have

$$H(2^k\omega)\Psi(2^{-(j-k)}\omega) = \gamma_j V(2^{-(j-k)}\omega). \tag{6.9}$$

In the other hand, directly plugging level index $j-k$ into (6.8) produces

$$H(\omega)\Psi(2^{-(j-k)}\omega) = \gamma_{j-k} V(2^{-(j-k)}\omega). \tag{6.10}$$

By comparing (6.9) and (6.10), we conclude that it must be true that

$$\frac{H(2^k\omega)}{H(\omega)} = \frac{\gamma_j}{\gamma_{j-k}} \ (independent\ of\ \omega) \,,$$

which is the characteristic of dilation-homogeneous operators in the frequency domain.

6.3 Discrete-time Overcomplete Wavelet Packet Inversion

6.3.1 One-dimensional Formulation

There were two major considerations in our searching for a deblurring algorithm. First, it should be available in the discrete-time domain. Second, it should be applicable to inhomogeneous blurring operators. The result was the discrete-time overcomplete wavelet packet representations equipped with a nonlinear shrinking operator and a gain operator. For an one-dimensional observation $y(k) = d(k) * x(k) + n(k)$, our deblurring algorithm can be expressed by:

$$w_j(k) = \sum_{m=-\infty}^{\infty} v_j(m)y(k - m), \qquad (6.11)$$

$$x'(k) = \sum_{j=0}^{M-1} \sum_{m=-\infty}^{\infty} \mathcal{K}_{t_j}\left[w_j(m)\right]\lambda_j u_j(k - m), \qquad (6.12)$$

where $\{\lambda_j|_{0\leq j\leq M-1}\}$ is the gain vector and $\mathcal{K}_{t_j}$ is the shrinking operator. Notice that for shrinking operators defined by (4.4) it is easy to show

$$\mathcal{K}_{t_j}\left[w_j(m)\right]\lambda_j = \mathcal{K}_{|\lambda_j|t_j}\left[w_j(m)\lambda_j\right],$$

which means that the order of gain and shrinking operator can be exchanged. If the shrinking threshold is adaptive to magnitude of coefficients, such a change of order would not alter the result. We prefer the order of "denoising" and then "inversing" as expressed in (6.12) over the order of "inversing" and then "denoising" of (6.7) since we believed the former is more logical.

The idea behind our method is the same as in the WVD inversion (6.7). That is to cut off noise by nonlinear means and then sharpen the survived coefficients. Although the formula (6.12) looks virtually the same as the WVD inversion, it has several major differences. First, it uses discrete-time overcomplete wavelet packet representation, which guarantees it will not fall on the anomaly of aliasing enhancement. Second, its analyzing and synthesizing functions do not subject to the dyadic bandwidth constraint, and do not necessarily satisfy the quasi-singular value relations (Eqs. (6.5) and (6.6)).

To complete the framework, we still need to resolve two issues. First, for a given blur with frequency response $D(\omega)$, how can we determine the channel configuration (analyzing and synthesizing filters) as well as the gain vector? Second, how should we choose thresholds t_j for denoising?

We proposed the following algorithm for the channel structure and the gain vector:

1) Choose a gain-limited inverse filter or a Wiener filter to approximate.

2) Choose the prototype filters $H(\omega)$, $\widetilde{H}(\omega)$, $G(\omega)$ and $\widetilde{G}(\omega)$, and then the channel filters of the Level 1 can be determined by $C_{1,0}(\omega) = H(\omega)\widetilde{H}(\omega)$ and $C_{1,1}(\omega) = G(\omega)\widetilde{G}(\omega)$.

3) Call Algorithm 4.2.2 (Minimum Tree) to determine both the tree configuration and gain vector.

However, the issue of determining thresholds t_j of denoising is much more difficult. Thresholding schemes for several particular applications were suggested by Donoho [15]. Generally speaking, knowledge about signals and noise is needed to devise a thresholding scheme. By treating signal and noise as two random processes, the correlation property may be used to characterize them, as in the case of Wiener filtering. For wide-sense stationary *white* Gaussian noise and *colored* Gaussian signals, their autocorrelation functions ϕ and power spectrum densities Φ may be written as:

$$\phi_{nn}(m) = \sigma_n^2\delta(m), \quad \Phi_{nn}(\omega) = \sigma_n^2,$$
$$\phi_{xx}(m) = ae^{-(m/\sigma_x)^2}, \quad \Phi_{xx}(\omega) \approx a\sqrt{\frac{\pi}{2}}\sigma_x^2 e^{-(\omega/\sigma_x)^2} \tag{6.13}$$

Note that $\Phi_{xx}(\omega)$ is generally different from the power density spectrum $|X(\omega)|^2$ of a particular realization x of the signal process. Under these assumptions, a possible thresholding scheme is:

$$t_j = \alpha\sqrt{\sigma_n^2 B_j/\Phi_{xx}(\omega_j)}, \tag{6.14}$$

where B_j is the bandwidth of the channel j, and ω_j is the center frequency of the channel.

6.3.2 Two-dimensional Extension

The one-dimensional algorithm of the overcomplete wavelet packet inversion need to be extended to two-dimension in order to deal with images degraded by *symmetric* 2D blurs. Formally, the 2D version may be written as

$$x'(k_1, k_2) = \sum_{c_1=0}^{M-1} \sum_{c_2=0}^{M-1} \sum_{m_1} \sum_{m_2} \mathcal{K}_{t_{c_1,c_2}}[w_{c_1,c_2}(m_1, m_2)] \lambda_{c_1,c_2} u_{c_1,c_2}(k_1 - m_1, k_2 - m_2).$$

However, an efficient 2D overcomplete wavelet packet representation is much more difficult to seek than in the 1D cases. In general, the 2D separable overcomplete wavelet packets may not be the efficient representation. This is due to the fact that both 2D modified inverse filters and Wiener filters are non-separable even for separable symmetric 2D blurs. For example, for a separable Gaussian blur:

$$D(\omega_x, \omega_y) = A e^{-(\omega_x^2 + \omega_y^2)/\sigma^2},$$

the pseudo-inverse filter and the Wiener filter are

$$F(\omega_x, \omega_y) = \begin{cases} 1/A \; e^{(\omega_x^2 + \omega_y^2)/\sigma^2} & , \sqrt{\omega_x^2 + \omega_y^2} \le \sigma \sqrt{\ln(A/R)} \\ 0 & , otherwise, \end{cases} \tag{6.15}$$

and

$$F(\omega_x, \omega_y) = 1/\left(1 + R/A \; e^{(\omega_x^2 + \omega_y^2)/\sigma^2}\right).$$

Both filters are isotropic and can be efficiently represented by donut-shaped channel filters.

In practice, a reasonable approximation may be achieved by applying the 1D algorithm separately to rows and columns. For the separable Gaussian blur, a separable pseudo-inverse filter may be constructed as:

$$F(\omega_x, \omega_y) = F_1(\omega_x) F_1(\omega_y),$$

where the 1D filter $F_1(\omega)$ is

$$F_1(\omega) = \begin{cases} \sqrt{1/A}\ e^{\omega^2/\sigma^2} &, |\omega| \le \sigma\sqrt{\ln(A/R)} \\ 0 &, \textit{otherwise}. \end{cases}$$

It is clear that the rectangular region $(|\omega_x| \le \sigma\sqrt{\ln(A/R)}, |\omega_y| \le \sigma\sqrt{\ln(A/R)})$ of the above 2D filter includes the disk of $\sqrt{\omega_x^2 + \omega_y^2} \le \sigma\sqrt{\ln(A/R)}$ of the (6.15). By choosing appropriate parameter R, acceptable results may also be achieved by approximating 2D Wiener filters with 1D Wiener filters. For uniform blurs, gain-limited inverse filters are similar to Wiener filters.

The major problem of such separable approximations is they may boost diagonal frequency components significantly. Figures 6.1 and 6.2 show examples of both 2D non-separable and separable filters. The emphasis of the diagonal frequency region is particularly clear in the case of Gaussian blur.

6.4 Experimental Results

To quantitatively compare deblurring results, we used an objective measure, the improvement in signal-to-noise ratio (ISNR), defined as [3]:

$$ISNR_p = 20\log\left\{\frac{\|x-y\|_p}{\|x-x'\|_p}\right\}, \ p = 1, 2 ,$$

where $\|v\|_p$ is L_p norm defined as [56]:

$$\|v\|_p = \left(\sum_{n=0}^{N-1} |v(n)|^p\right)^{1/p},$$

and x, y and x' are the original, degraded and deblurred signals, respectively.

Moreover, a performance upper bound is useful in providing a gauge for comparison. The performance of an oracle Wiener filter may be considered the upper bound for Wiener filters. An oracle Wiener filter is a Wiener filter with $\Phi_{nn}(\omega)$ and $\Phi_{xx}(\omega)$ replaced by power density spectrums $|N(\omega)|^2$ and $|X(\omega)|^2$ of the particular realization of the noise and the original signal. The filter may be written as:

$$F(\omega) = \frac{D^*(\omega)}{|D(\omega)|^2 + |N(\omega)|^2 / |X(\omega)|^2} .$$

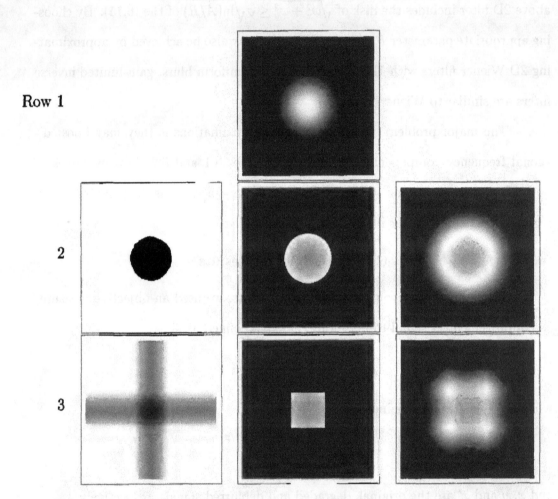

Row 1

2

3

Figure 6.1: Log Frequency Responses of Filters for a Gaussian Blur.
Where:

    Row 1: Blurring filter

    Row 2: 2D non-separable filters, gain-limited, pseudo-inverse and
             Wiener filter from left to right

    Row 3: 2D separable filters, gain-limited, pseudo-inverse and
             Wiener filter from left to right

Row 1

2

3

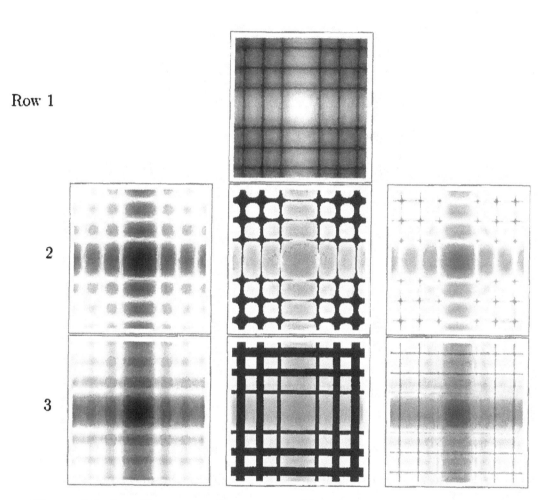

Figure 6.2: Log Frequency Responses of Filters for an Uniform Blur.
Where:

Row 1: Blurring filter

Row 2: 2D non-separable filters, gain-limited, pseudo-inverse and
Wiener filter from left to right

Row 3: 2D separable filters, gain-limited, pseudo-inverse and
Wiener filter from left to right

However, it is not necessarily the upper bound of the overcomplete wavelet packet inversion.

6.4.1 One-dimensional Signals

One-dimensional deblurring examples are shown in Figure 6.3 and 6.4. The ideal signal in both cases is a perfect multi-level blocky function, which is very challenging and revealing for any deblurring method. For overcomplete wavelet packet representations used in both examples, Lemarié filter of $p=1$ was used. In Figure 6.3, the impulse response of a Gaussian blur was:

$$f(k) = \begin{cases} A \exp\left[-(k/(\sigma N/2))^2\right], & 0 \le k \le N/2, \\ A \exp\left[-((N-k)/(\sigma N/2))^2\right], & N/2 < k < N, \end{cases}$$

with $\sigma = 0.03$ and $A = 1.0/\sum_k f(k)$. The impulse response of the uniform blur was $f = [1,1,1,1,1,1,1]/7$. In both cases, white noise with $\sigma_n^2 = 0.01$ was added such that the ratio of peak signal power to average noise power was $SNR = 10\log(x_{max}^2/\sigma_n^2)$ $= 21.6db$. To make fair comparisons, the same Gaussian signal model of (6.13) with $a = 1.0$ and $\sigma_x = 0.007$ was used for both Wiener filtering and the overcomplete wavelet packet inversion. The thresholding scheme of (6.14) with $\alpha = 0.25$ and $\alpha = 0.18$ was used for the Gaussian and uniform blur, respectively. The gain-limited inverse filter (6.1) with $R = 0.04$ and $R = 0.05$ was used for the Gaussian and uniform blur, respectively. For the minimum tree algorithm, the maximum depth was set to Level 6. The algorithm found a configuration of twenty-five channels with $\varepsilon = 5.7\%$ in the case of uniform blur, and twelve channels with $\varepsilon = 0.004\%$ in the case of Gaussian blur.

Table 6.1 compares deblurring performance in terms of $ISNR$. For the two *particular* blurring sources and the signal, it shows that overall performance of the overcomplete wavelet packet inversion is about the same as Wiener filtering by the measure of $ISNR_2$, and it is better than Wiener filtering by $ISNR_1$.

Row 1

2

3

4

5

6

7

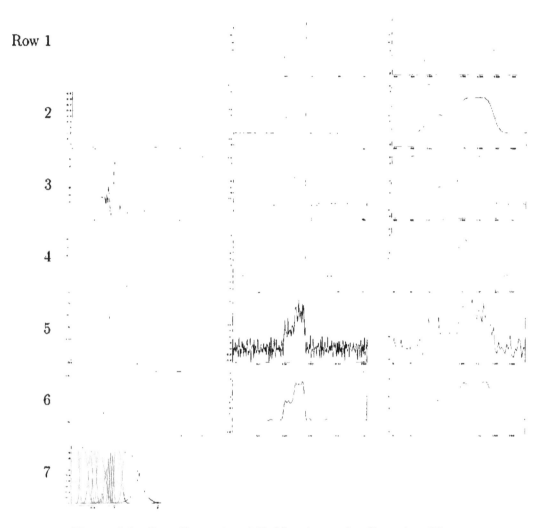

Figure 6.3: One-dimensional Deblurrings of a Gaussian Blur.
Where:

Row 1: The original signal

Row 2: The blur filter and the degraded signal

Row 3: The oracle Wiener filter and the deblurred signal

Row 4: The Wiener filter and the deblurred signal

Row 5: The gain-limited inverse filter and the deblurred signal

Row 6: The overall frequency response of the overcomplete wavelet packet inversion and the deblurred signal

Row 7: Channels of the overcomplete wavelet packet representation

Note: The left column are frequency responses. The central column are signals of full-length. The right column are zoom-in of the feature region, where deblurring results were overlaid with the degraded signal of doted line.

Row 1

2

3

4

5

6

7

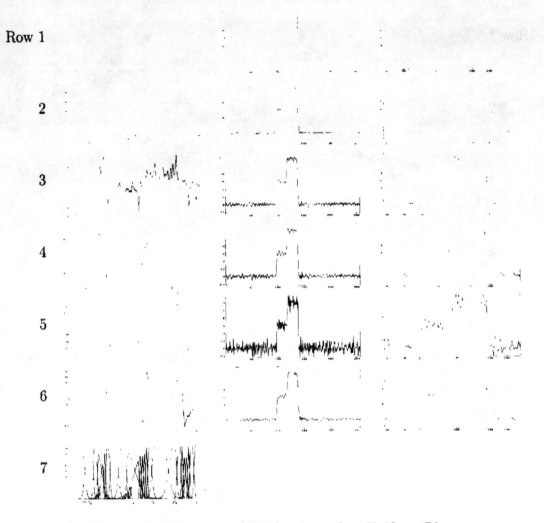

Figure 6.4: One-dimensional Deblurrings of an Uniform Blur.
Where:

    Row 1: The original signal

    Row 2: The blur filter and the degraded signal

    Row 3: The oracle Wiener filter and the deblurred signal

    Row 4: The Wiener filter and the deblurred signal

    Row 5: The gain-limited inverse filter and the deblurred signal

    Row 6: The overall frequency response of the overcomplete wavelet
          packet inversion and the deblurred signal

    Row 7: Channels of the overcomplete wavelet packet representation

Note: The left column are frequency responses. The central column
are signals of full-length. The right column are zoom-in of the feature
region, where deblurring results were overlaid with the degraded signal
of doted line.

Table 6.1: Performance of 1D Deblurring Examples

Blur Type	$ISNR_2$ (DB)				$ISNR_1$ (DB)			
	OWF	WF	GLIF	OWPI	OWF	WF	GLIF	OWPI
Gaussian	2.37	1.88	-9.04	1.90	-0.75	-1.45	-15.87	1.18
Uniform	5.17	3.90	-4.32	3.62	-1.00	-2.40	-11.80	0.00

Note:

OWF=Oracle Wiener Filter
WF=Wiener Filter
GLIF=Gain-limited Inverse Filter
OWPI=Overcomplete Wavelet Packet Inversion

6.4.2 Two-dimensional Images

Examples of image deblurring using the standard Lena image were included in Figures 6.5 and 6.6. Separable blurring sources were used. The same 1D blurring filters used in the 1D examples were applied row-wise and column-wise on the original Lena image. A statistical signal model of (6.13) with $a = 3.5$ and $\sigma_x = 0.008$ was used for both Wiener filtering and the overcomplete wavelet packet inversion. In both cases, white Gaussian noise with $\sigma_n^2 = 0.5$ was added such that $SNR = 44.3DB$. The thresholding scheme of (6.14) with $\alpha = 25.2$ was used for both cases. The shrinking operator was applied on the 2D components. The gain-limited inverse filter (6.1) with $R = 0.08$ was used for both comparison and overcomplete wavelet packet inversion. A separable overcomplete wavelet packet inversion algorithm was used to approximate a 2D overcomplete wavelet packet inversion. For the case of Gaussian blur, the approximation used 11×11 channels with $\varepsilon = 0.005\%$ (1D). For the case of uniform blur, the approximation used 25×25 channels with $\varepsilon = 3.9\%$ (1D). The deblurred images were all linear converted to the same intensity range of the original image for the calculation of $ISNR$ indexes.

Table 6.2 compares deblurring performance in terms of $ISNR$. For the two *particular* blurring sources and the Lena image, it shows that overall performance of

Table 6.2: Performance of 2D Deblurring Examples

Blur Type	$ISNR_2$ (DB)				$ISNR_1$ (DB)			
	OWF	WF	GLIF	OWPI	OWF	WF	GLIF	OWPI
Gaussian	3.20	3.17	-14.04	2.80	2.96	3.25	-16.82	2.69
Uniform	3.55	1.78	-14.78	1.76	1.46	-0.60	-18.05	-0.64

Note:

OWF=Oracle Wiener Filter
WF=Wiener Filter
GLIF=Gain-limited Inverse Filter
OWPI=Overcomplete Wavelet Packet Inversion

the overcomplete wavelet packet inversion is about the same as Wiener filtering by both measures of $ISNR_2$ and $ISNR_1$.

6.5   Summary and Discussion

We have demonstrated that the deblurring problem can be handled using an overcomplete wavelet packet representation. We showed that inverse filtering in the frequency domain and denoising in the time domain can be done in a single step. In other words, for this application the gain and shrinking operators can be combined as a single operation on the spatial-frequency representation. Moreover, our approach may be seen as an extension of the wavelet-vaguelette inversion into both the discrete-time and broader problem domains.

Although the one step inversion and denoising may be conceptually appealing, its limitation is also apparent. Since nonlinear shrinkage works only within areas where the magnitude of signal components is stronger than that of noise components, the best representation for denoising is to maximize local signal-to-noise ratio. For example, if a sharp edge is decomposed into many channels, its components at some channels may be indistinguishable from noise. Therefore, the best representations for approximating the inverse filter and denoising are generally different. Having only one choice of representation, the approach has to limit its application to certain signals or blurring sources.

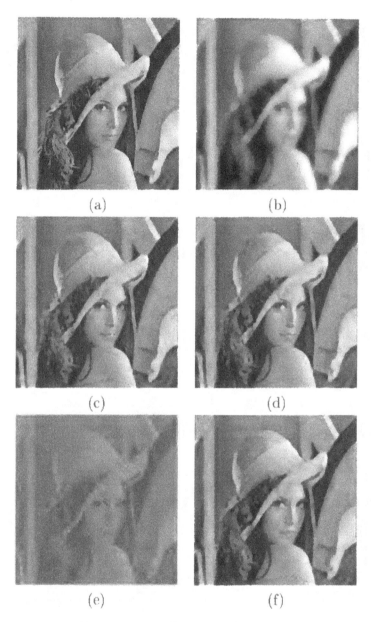

Figure 6.5: Deblurring a Gaussian-blurred Lena Image.

Legend:

(a) The original 256×256 image

(b) Degraded image with SNR=44.3 db

(c) Deblurred by the oracle Wiener filter

(d) Deblurred by a Wiener filter

(e) Deblurred by a gain-limited inverse filter

(f) Deblurred by a separable overcomplete wavelet packet inversion

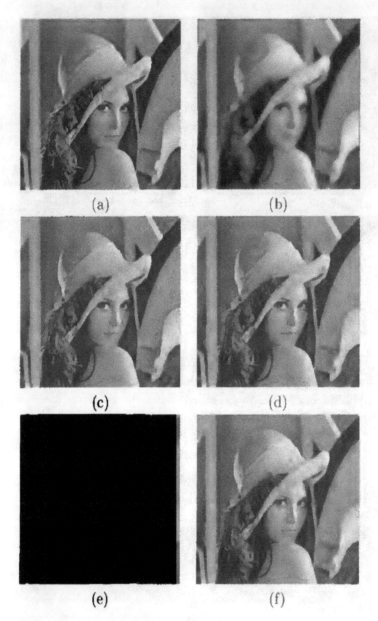

Figure 6.6: Deblurring an Uniform-blurred Lena Image.

Legend:

(a) The original 256×256 image

(b) Degraded image with SNR=44.3 db

(c) Deblurred by the oracle Wiener filter

(d) Deblurred by a Wiener filter

(e) Deblurred by a gain-limited inverse filter

(f) Deblurred by a separable overcomplete wavelet packet inversion

This limitation may be the reason that our preliminary experimental results showed roughly the same performance as the much simpler approach of the Wiener filtering. For the Gaussian and uniform blurring sources, some channels with very narrow bandwidth are needed to achieve satisfactory approximation using the gain vector. For those channels, shrinking operation is very close to multiplication.

CHAPTER 7
CONCLUSION

We examined both classes of Fourier-based and wavelet-based representations. We showed that orthogonal wavelet transforms lack translation invariance and the efficacy of representing convolution operators. In particular, we demonstrated that aliasing distortion due to critical subsampling limits its applications in image enhancement and restoration. On the other hand, overcomplete wavelet representations, although not as efficient as non-redundant representations, avoid those shortcomings. Moreover, overcomplete wavelet representations can be conveniently analyzed using linear time invariant system theory. In this thesis, we evaluated their capability of time-frequency localization using the uncertainty factor. We also identified gain, shrinking and envelope operators to approximate convolution operators, suppress noise and extract power density distributions. We investigated the criteria of minimum mean square error and designed an optimization algorithm. We extended the wavelet shrinkage to overcomplete representations. We also presented two envelope detection algorithms and compared their performances.

The framework of the overcomplete wavelet representation was applied to two difficult problems: segmentation of textured images and image deblurring. We demonstrated that channel envelopes as feature vector produced satisfactory results on both natural and synthetic textures. We showed the gain and shrinking operators may be used for image deblurring and pointed out its limitations.

The issues of time-frequency representations, pattern recognition and noise suppression are very fundamental ones. Our knowledge about them is going to be accumulative and evolving. This thesis increases our level of understanding and points

86

to many opportunities for future research. The issue of time-frequency localization was touched upon but not fully explored. Although the uncertainty factor was used for evaluation of individual channels, we lack a criteria of optimality on a representation as a whole. Once such a criteria is found, we may able to search for the optimal representation of textured images, which was not explored here. Denoising is certainly another front. The optimal representation and adaptive selection of thresholds are going to be intertwined and challenging.

APPENDIX A
PROOFS RELATED TO DISCRETE-TIME WAVELETS

Some basic proofs related to (bi)orthogonal discrete-time wavelets were included here in order to make this thesis self-sustained.

Proposition A.0.1 *The necessary condition for a pair of discrete sequences to be orthogonal (as defined by (A.1)) is (A.2):*

$$\sum_{m=-\infty}^{\infty} a(2n-m)b(m-2l) = \lambda\delta(n-l) \qquad (A.1)$$

$$\Longrightarrow$$

$$A(e^{j\omega})B(e^{j\omega}) + A(e^{j(\omega+\pi)})B(e^{j(\omega+\pi)}) = 2\lambda, \qquad (A.2)$$

where λ is a constant, and $A(e^{j\omega})$ and $B(e^{j\omega})$ are discrete-time Fourier transform of $a(n)$ and $b(n)$, respectively.

Proof: By changing variable $k = m - 2l$, the left side of (A.1) is changed to $\sum_{k=-\infty}^{\infty} a\left[2(n-l) - k\right] b(k)$. Then it is equivalent to prove that

$$\sum_{k=-\infty}^{\infty} a(2l-k)b(k) = \lambda\delta(l).$$

Notice that the left side of the above is a 2-fold decimation of the series

$$p(l) = \sum_{k=-\infty}^{\infty} a(l-k)b(k).$$

Since $p(l)$ is the convolution of $a(l)$ and $b(l)$, its discrete-time Fourier transform is known as

$$P(e^{j\omega}) = A(e^{j\omega})B(e^{j\omega}).$$

88

Using the result on M-fold decimator proved in [63], Fourier transform of $p(2l)$ is equal to

$$\frac{1}{2}\left[P(e^{j\omega/2}) + P(e^{j(\omega+2\pi)/2})\right],$$

and therefore the Fourier transform of (A.1) is

$$P(e^{j\omega/2}) + P(e^{j(\omega+2\pi)/2}) = 2\lambda.$$

Finally, by substituting $P(e^{j\omega}) = A(e^{j\omega})B(e^{j\omega})$ back, we proved

$$A(e^{j\omega/2})B(e^{j\omega/2}) + A(e^{j(\omega+2\pi)/2})B(e^{j(\omega+2\pi)/2}) = 2\lambda \quad \blacksquare$$

Proposition A.0.2 *The necessary condition for (A.3) is (A.4):*

$$\sum_{l=-\infty}^{\infty} a(2l-m)b(n-2l) + \sum_{l=-\infty}^{\infty} c(2l-m)d(n-2l) = \delta(m-n) \qquad (A.3)$$

$$\Longrightarrow$$

$$\left.\begin{aligned} A(e^{j\omega})B(e^{j\omega}) + C(e^{j\omega})D(e^{j\omega}) &= 2. \\ A(e^{j\omega})B(e^{j(\omega+\pi)}) + C(e^{j\omega})D(e^{j(\omega+\pi)}) &= 0. \end{aligned}\right\} \qquad (A.4)$$

Proof: Consider both sides of (A.3) to be two-dimensional series of index (m, n), and apply two-dimensional Fourier transform to the both sides.

Let $p(m, n) = \sum_{l=-\infty}^{\infty} a(2l-m)b(n-2l)$, then

$$
\begin{aligned}
P(e^{j\omega_x}, e^{j\omega_y}) &= \sum_{m=-\infty}^{\infty} \sum_{n=-\infty}^{\infty} p(m, n)e^{-jm\omega_x}e^{-jn\omega_y} \\
&= \sum_{l=-\infty}^{\infty} \left[\sum_{m=-\infty}^{\infty} a(2l-m)e^{-jm\omega_x}\right]\left[\sum_{n=-\infty}^{\infty} b(n-2l)e^{-jn\omega_y}\right] \\
&= \left[\sum_{l=-\infty}^{\infty} e^{-jl(2\omega_x+2\omega_y)}\right]\left[\sum_{m=-\infty}^{\infty} a(m)e^{jm\omega_x}\right]\left[\sum_{n=-\infty}^{\infty} b(n)e^{-jn\omega_y}\right] \\
&= \sum_{k=-\infty}^{\infty} 2\pi\delta(2\omega_x + 2\omega_y + 2k\pi)A(e^{-j\omega_x})B(e^{j\omega_y}) \\
&= \sum_{k=-\infty}^{\infty} \pi\delta(\omega_x + \omega_y + k\pi)A(e^{-j\omega_x})B(e^{j\omega_y})
\end{aligned}
$$

Therefore, the 2D Fourier transform of the left side is

$$\sum_{k=-\infty}^{\infty} \pi\delta(\omega_x + \omega_y + k\pi) \left[A(e^{-j\omega_x})B(e^{j\omega_y}) + C(e^{-j\omega_x})D(e^{j\omega_y}) \right]$$

and that of the right side is

$$\sum_{m=-\infty}^{\infty} \sum_{n=-\infty}^{\infty} \delta(m-n)e^{-jm\omega_x}e^{-jn\omega_y} = \sum_{n=-\infty}^{\infty} e^{-jn(\omega_x+\omega_y)}$$

$$= \sum_{k=-\infty}^{\infty} 2\pi\delta(\omega_x + \omega_y + 2k\pi).$$

Thus, 2D Fourier transform of (A.3) is

$$\sum_{k=-\infty}^{\infty} \delta(\omega_x + \omega_y + k\pi) \left[A(e^{-j\omega_x})B(e^{j\omega_y}) + C(e^{-j\omega_x})D(e^{j\omega_y}) \right]$$

$$= \sum_{k=-\infty}^{\infty} 2\delta(\omega_x + \omega_y + 2k\pi).$$

By combining terms with even and odd index of k, the above equation can be rewritten as

$$\sum_{k=-\infty}^{\infty} \delta(\omega_x + \omega_y + 2k\pi) \left[X(e^{j\omega_x}, e^{j\omega_y}) - 2 \right]$$

$$+ \quad \sum_{k=-\infty}^{\infty} \delta\left(\omega_x + \omega_y + (2k+1)\pi\right) X(e^{j\omega_x}, e^{j\omega_y}) = 0,$$

where

$$X(e^{j\omega_x}, e^{j\omega_y}) = A(e^{-j\omega_x})B(e^{j\omega_y}) + C(e^{-j\omega_x})D(e^{j\omega_y}).$$

Using the properties of the δ function, the coefficients of the above δ series must satisfy

$$X(e^{-j(\omega+2k\pi)}, e^{j\omega}) = X(e^{-j\omega}, e^{j\omega}) = 2,$$

$$X(e^{-j(\omega+(2k+1)\pi)}, e^{j\omega}) = X(e^{-j(\omega+\pi)}, e^{j\omega}) = 0.$$

Finally, by substituting $X(e^{j\omega_x}, e^{j\omega_y})$ back, we proved

$$A(e^{j\omega})B(e^{j\omega}) + C(e^{j\omega})D(e^{j\omega}) = 2,$$

$$A(e^{j(\omega+\pi)})B(e^{j\omega}) + C(e^{j(\omega+\pi)})D(e^{j\omega}) = 0 \quad \blacksquare$$

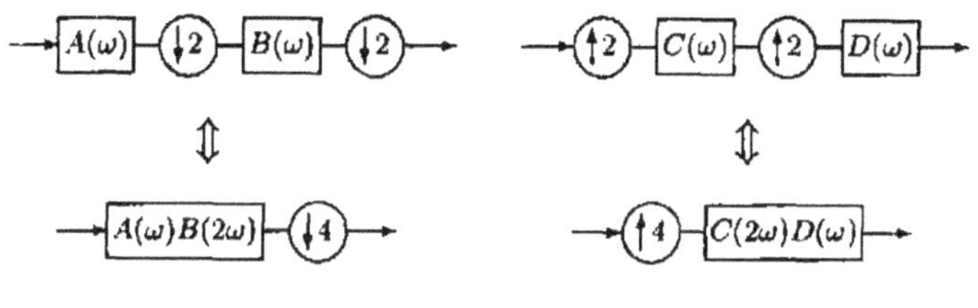

Figure A.1: Equivalent Structures for (a) Convolution and Decimation and (b) Expansion and Convolution.

Proposition A.0.3 *Two cascaded stages of convolution and decimation (expansion) are equivalent to a single stage convolution and decimation (expansion) as illustrated in Figure A.1.*

Proof: Assume input $x(n)$ and output $y(n)$, and $a(n)$ and $b(n)$ are the inverse DFT of $A(\omega)$ and $B(\omega)$.

For (a),

$$
\begin{aligned}
y(n) &= \sum_{m=-\infty}^{\infty} \left[\sum_{k=-\infty}^{\infty} x(k)a(2m-k) \right] b(2n-m) \\
&= \sum_{k=-\infty}^{\infty} x(k) \left[\sum_{m=-\infty}^{\infty} a(2m-k)b(2n-m) \right] \\
&= \sum_{k=-\infty}^{\infty} x(k) \left[\sum_{l=-\infty}^{\infty} a(4n-k-2l)b(l) \right] \\
&= \sum_{k=-\infty}^{\infty} x(k)p(4n-k)
\end{aligned}
$$

where $p(n) = \sum_{l=-\infty}^{\infty} a(n-2l)b(l)$, or $P(e^{j\omega}) = A(e^{j\omega})B(e^{j2\omega})$.

Similarly, for (b),

$$
\begin{aligned}
y(n) &= \sum_{m=-\infty}^{\infty} \left[\sum_{k=-\infty}^{\infty} x(k)c(m-2k) \right] d(n-2m) \\
&= \sum_{k=-\infty}^{\infty} x(k) \left[\sum_{m=-\infty}^{\infty} c(m-2k)d(n-2m) \right] \\
&= \sum_{k=-\infty}^{\infty} x(k) \left[\sum_{l=-\infty}^{\infty} c(l)d(n-4k-2l) \right] \\
&= \sum_{k=-\infty}^{\infty} x(k)q(n-4k)
\end{aligned}
$$

where $q(n) = \sum_{l=-\infty}^{\infty} c(l)d(n-2l)$, or $Q(e^{j\omega}) = C(e^{j2\omega})D(e^{j\omega})$ ∎

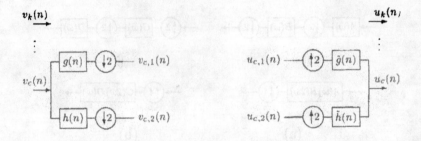

Figure A.2: Illustration of Adding One More Channel by Splitting a Channel into Two.

Proposition A.0.4 *The basis functions for a binary tree structured filter bank can be expressed as:*

$$V_0(e^{j\omega}) = G(e^{j\omega}), \qquad U_0(e^{j\omega}) = \tilde{G}(e^{j\omega}), \qquad k = 0$$

$$V_k(e^{j\omega}) = \prod_{l=0}^{k-1} H(e^{j2^l\omega})G(e^{j2^k\omega}), \quad U_k(e^{j\omega}) = \prod_{l=0}^{k-1} \tilde{H}(e^{j2^l\omega})\tilde{G}(e^{j2^k\omega}), \quad 1 \le k \le M-2$$

$$V_{M-1}(e^{j\omega}) = \prod_{l=0}^{M-1} H(e^{j2^l\omega}), \qquad U_{M-1}(e^{j\omega}) = \prod_{l=0}^{M-1} \tilde{H}(e^{j2^l\omega}), \qquad k = M-1.$$

where $M \ge 2$.

For orthogonal wavelet basis satisfying condition (2.11), we have

$$U_k(e^{j\omega}) = V_k^*(e^{j\omega}), \quad or, \quad u_k(n) = v_k^*(-n).$$

Proof: By direct application of the Proposition A.0.3. ∎

Proposition A.0.5 *Basis functions generated by a general binary tree with filters $h_i(n)$ and $g_i(n)$ satisfying (2.9) satisfy the following biorthogonality:*

$$\sum_{m=-\infty}^{\infty} u_c(m - n_c l)v_k(n_k n - m) = \delta(c - k)\delta(l - n) \qquad (A.5)$$

Proof: By induction. For filter bank of 2 channels, $u_0 = \tilde{g}_0(n)$, $u_1 = \tilde{h}_0(n)$, $v_0 = g_0(n)$ and $v_1 = h_0(n)$. In this case, the orthonomality of the basis functions is the given property. Now, assume (A.5) is true for up to M channels. To construct a $M+1$ channel filter bank, we split an arbitrary channel c into two as illustrated in Figure A.2.

Since transform coefficient $w_c(n)$ before splitting is

$$w_c(n) = \sum_{m=-\infty}^{\infty} x(m)v_c(n_c n - m),$$

the new coefficient $w_{c1}(n)$ and $w_{c2}(n)$ are

$$
\begin{aligned}
w_{c1}(n) &= \sum_{l=-\infty}^{\infty} w_c(l)g_c(2n - l) \\
&= \sum_{m=-\infty}^{\infty} x(m)\left[\sum_{l=-\infty}^{\infty} v_c(n_c l - m)g_c(2n - l)\right] \\
&= \sum_{m=-\infty}^{\infty} x(m)v_{c1}(2n_c n - m),
\end{aligned}
$$

where $v_{c1}(n) = \sum_{l=-\infty}^{\infty} v_c(n - n_c l)g_c(l)$.

Similarly,

$$v_{c2}(n) = \sum_{l=-\infty}^{\infty} v_c(n - n_c l)h_c(l),$$

$$u_{c1}(n) = \sum_{l=-\infty}^{\infty} u_c(n - n_c l)\tilde{g}_c(l),$$

$$u_{c2}(n) = \sum_{l=-\infty}^{\infty} u_c(n - n_c l)\tilde{h}_c(l).$$

For $k \neq c1$ and $k \neq c2$

$$
\begin{aligned}
&\sum_{m=-\infty}^{\infty} u_{c1}(m - n_{c1}i)v_k(n_k n - m) \\
&= \sum_{m=-\infty}^{\infty}\left[\sum_{l=-\infty}^{\infty} u_c(m - 2n_c i - n_c l)\tilde{g}_c(l)\right]v_k(n_k n - m) \\
&= \sum_{l=-\infty}^{\infty} \tilde{g}_c(l)\left[\sum_{m=-\infty}^{\infty} u_c(m - n_c(2i - l))v_k(n_k n - m)\right] \\
&= \sum_{l=-\infty}^{\infty} \tilde{g}_c(l)\delta(c - k)\delta(2i - l - n) = 0.
\end{aligned}
$$

and similarly,

$$\sum_{m=-\infty}^{\infty} u_{c2}(m - n_{c1}i)v_k(n_k n - m) = 0.$$

For $k = c1$,

$$
\begin{aligned}
&\sum_{m=-\infty}^{\infty} u_{c1}(m - n_{c1}i)v_{c1}(n_{c1}n - m) \\
&= \sum_{m=-\infty}^{\infty}\left[\sum_{l_1=-\infty}^{\infty} u_c(m - 2n_c i - n_c l_1)\tilde{g}_c(l_1)\right]\left[\sum_{l_2=-\infty}^{\infty} v_c(2n_c n - m - n_c l_2)g_c(l_2)\right] \\
&= \sum_{l_1=-\infty}^{\infty}\sum_{l_2=-\infty}^{\infty} \tilde{g}_c(l_1)g_c(l_2)\left[\sum_{m=-\infty}^{\infty} u_c(m - n_c(2i + l_1))v_c(n_c(2n - l_2) - m)\right] \\
&= \sum_{l_1=-\infty}^{\infty}\sum_{l_2=-\infty}^{\infty} \tilde{g}_c(l_1)g_c(l_2)\delta(2i + l_1 - 2n + l_2) \\
&= \sum_{l_1=-\infty}^{\infty} \tilde{g}_c(l_1)g_c(2(n - i) - l_1) \stackrel{(2.9)}{=} \delta(n - i).
\end{aligned}
$$

Similarly, we can prove

$$\sum_{m=-\infty}^{\infty} u_{c2}(m - n_{c1}i)v_{c2}(n_{c1}n - m) = \delta(n - i),$$
$$\sum_{m=-\infty}^{\infty} u_{c1}(m - n_{c1}i)v_{c2}(n_{c1}n - m) = 0,$$
$$\sum_{m=-\infty}^{\infty} u_{c2}(m - n_{c1}i)v_{c1}(n_{c1}n - m) = 0 \quad \blacksquare$$

We have thus proved that basis functions of the new filter bank constructed this way are also orthonomal. Notice that orthonomality hold under quite general conditions:

1) Filters g_c, h_c, $\tilde{g}_c$ and $\bar{h}_c$ may be different with those used in other channels, as long as they satisfy condition (2.9).

2) Splitting can be done arbitrarily.

APPENDIX B
NUMERICAL COMPUTATION OF BATTLE-LEMARIÉ WAVELET

Battle-Lemarié wavelets are built from polynomial spline of order $2p+1$ [42]. Although they are not compactly supported, they do possess two important properties: symmetric and orthogonal. The symmetric property is especially desirable for some image processing applications such as edge detection, character recognition [39], and texture segmentation [62], but is mutual exclusive with the compact support property [13].

In this appendix, we presented an algorithm to compute the scaling function, wavelet, and associated quadrature mirror filters of Battle-Lemarié wavelets.

B.1 Functions in Finite Terms

The Fourier transform of the scaling function ϕ, wavelet ψ, and the associated quadrature mirror filter h may be written as [42]:

$$\Phi_p(\omega) \;=\; \frac{1}{\omega^{2p+2}\sqrt{\Sigma_{4p+4}(\omega)}} \tag{B.1}$$

$$\Psi_p(\omega) \;=\; \frac{e^{-j\frac{\omega}{2}}}{\omega^{2p+2}}\sqrt{\frac{\Sigma_{4p+4}(\frac{\omega}{2}+\pi)}{\Sigma_{4p+4}(\omega)\Sigma_{4p+4}(\frac{\omega}{2})}} \tag{B.2}$$

$$H_p(\omega) \;=\; \sqrt{\frac{\Sigma_{4p+4}(\omega)}{2^{4p+4}\Sigma_{4p+4}(2\omega)}} \tag{B.3}$$

where p is a positive integer and

$$\Sigma_n(\omega) = \sum_{k=-\infty}^{+\infty} \frac{1}{(\omega+2k\pi)^n}.$$

95

Therefore, the computation of the function $\Sigma_n(\omega)$ is the key. Fortunately, we have a closed form for $n = 2$ [42],

$$\Sigma_2(\omega) = \sum_{k=-\infty}^{+\infty} \frac{1}{(\omega + 2k\pi)^2} = \frac{1}{4\sin^2(\frac{\omega}{2})},$$

and a closed form expression of the function $\Sigma_n(\omega)$ based on $\Sigma_2(\omega)$:

$$\Sigma_n(\omega) = \frac{(-1)^n}{(n-1)!} \frac{d^{n-2}}{d\omega^{n-2}} \Sigma_2(\omega), \quad n > 2.$$

Thus, all we needed is an algorithm to compute derivatives of the function $\Sigma_2(\omega)$, which we shall derive in the following:

Proposition B.1.1 *For any integer $n \geq 1$, the nth order derivative of the function $\Sigma_2(\omega)$ has the form of*

$$\frac{d^n}{d\omega^n} \Sigma_2(\omega) = \frac{g_n(\cos \frac{\omega}{2})}{\sin^{n+2}(\frac{\omega}{2})}, \tag{B.4}$$

where $g_n(\cos \frac{\omega}{2})$ is a polynomial of order n and satisfied the following recursive relation:

$$g_{n+1}(x) = -\frac{1}{2} \frac{d\, g_n(x)}{dx}(1 - x^2) - \frac{(n+2)}{2} g_n(x) * x \tag{B.5}$$

Proof: By mathematical induction.

For $n = 1$, $\frac{d}{d\omega}\Sigma_2(\omega) = -0.25 \frac{\cos(\omega/2)}{\sin^3(\omega/2)}$. Thus, $g_1(\cos \omega/2) = -0.25 \cos(\omega/2)$. Assume for any $n > 1$, (B.4) is true, and $g_n(\cos \frac{\omega}{2})$ is a polynomial of order n. Then, for $n + 1$,

$$\frac{d^{n+1}\Sigma_2(\omega)}{d\omega^{n+1}} = \frac{d}{d\omega}\left(\frac{g_n(\cos \frac{\omega}{2})}{\sin^{n+2}(\frac{\omega}{2})}\right)$$

$$= \frac{\frac{d}{d\omega}\left(g_n(\cos \frac{\omega}{2})\right) * \sin^{n+2} - g_n(\cos \frac{\omega}{2}) * (n+2) * \sin^{n+1}(\frac{\omega}{2}) * \cos(\frac{\omega}{2}) * \frac{1}{2}}{\sin^{2n+4}(\frac{\omega}{2})}$$

$$= \frac{\frac{d}{d\cos \frac{\omega}{2}}\left(g_n(\cos \frac{\omega}{2})\right)\frac{d\cos \frac{\omega}{2}}{d\omega} * \sin \frac{\omega}{2} - \frac{(n+2)}{2} * g_n(\cos \frac{\omega}{2}) * \cos \frac{\omega}{2}}{\sin^{(n+1)+2}(\frac{\omega}{2})}$$

$$= \frac{-\frac{1}{2}\frac{d}{d\cos \frac{\omega}{2}} g_n(\cos \frac{\omega}{2}) * (1 - \cos^2 \frac{\omega}{2}) - \frac{(n+2)}{2} * g_n(\cos \frac{\omega}{2}) * \cos \frac{\omega}{2}}{\sin^{(n+1)+2}(\frac{\omega}{2})}$$

$$= \frac{g_{n+1}(\cos \frac{\omega}{2})}{\sin^{(n+1)+2}(\frac{\omega}{2})},$$

where $g_{n+1}(x) = -\frac{1}{2}\frac{d\,g_n(x)}{dx}(1-x^2) - \frac{(n+2)}{2}g_n(x)*x$, and is clearly of order $(n+1)$ ∎

Proposition B.1.2 *The coefficients $\{a_{n,k}\}$ of the polynomial $g_n(x)$ satisfies the following recursive relation:*

$$\left.\begin{array}{rcl}
a_{0,0} & = & 0.25 \\
a_{0,1} & = & 0 \\
a_{n,0} & = & -0.5a_{n-1,1} \\
a_{n,k} & = & 0.5\left[(k-n-2)a_{n-1,k-1} - (k+1)a_{n-1,k+1}\right], \ 1 \le k \le n-2 \\
a_{n,n-1} & = & -1.5a_{n-1,n-2} \\
a_{n,n} & = & -a_{n-1,n-1}
\end{array}\right\} \tag{B.6}$$

Proof: For $n = 0$, $a_{0,0} = 0.25$, $a_{0,1} = 0$. Based on Proposition B.1.1, we can write

$$g_{n-1}(x) = \sum_{k=0}^{n-1} a_{n-1,k}x^k$$

and,

$$g_n(x) = \sum_{k=0}^{n} a_{n,k}x^k \tag{B.7}$$

Using (B.5), we can derive

$$\begin{aligned}
g_n(x) &= -\frac{1}{2}\frac{d\,g_{n-1}(x)}{dx}(1-x^2) - \frac{(n+1)}{2}g_{n-1}(x)*x \\
&= -\frac{1}{2}\sum_{k=0}^{n-1}a_{n-1,k}kx^{k-1}*(1-x^2) - \frac{(n+1)}{2}\sum_{k=0}^{n-1}a_{n-1,k}x^{k+1} \\
&= -\frac{1}{2}\sum_{k=0}^{n-1}a_{n-1,k}kx^{k-1} + \frac{1}{2}\sum_{k=0}^{n-1}a_{n-1,k}kx^{k+1} - \frac{(n+1)}{2}\sum_{k=0}^{n-1}a_{n-1,k}x^{k+1} \\
&= -\frac{1}{2}\sum_{l=0}^{n-2}a_{n-1,l+1}*(l+1)*x^l + \frac{1}{2}\sum_{k=0}^{n-1}(k-n-1)*a_{n-1,k}x^{k+1} \\
&= -\frac{1}{2}a_{n-1,1} - \frac{1}{2}\sum_{l=1}^{n-2}a_{n-1,l+1}*(l+1)x^l + \frac{1}{2}\sum_{l=1}^{n}(l-n-2)*a_{n-1,l-1}x^l \\
&= -\frac{1}{2}a_{n-1,1} + \frac{1}{2}\sum_{l=1}^{n-2}\left[(l-n-2)*a_{n-1,l-1} - (l+1)a_{n-1,l+1}\right]x^l \\
&\quad -\frac{3}{2}a_{n-1,n-2}x^{n-1} - a_{n-1,n-1}x^n
\end{aligned} \tag{B.8}$$

Comparing (B.8) with (B.7), we obtain (B.6) ∎

Proposition B.1.3 *For even order n of the polynomial $g_n(x)$, only terms with an even index are nonzero. For odd order n of the polynomial $g_n(x)$, only odd index* *terms are nonzero. (This property halves the number of calculations needed for the coefficients.)*

Proof: By induction.

For $n = 1$, $a_{1,0} = -0.5a_{0,1} = 0$, $a_{1,1} = -a_{0,0} = -0.25$.

For $n = 2$, $a_{2,0} = -0.5a_{1,1} = 0.125$, $a_{2,1} = -1.5a_{1,0} = 0$, $a_{2,2} = -a_{1,1} = 0.25$.

Assume for $n - 1$, the assertion is valid.

For even n, let $n = 2m$,

$$
\begin{aligned}
a_{2m,0} &= -0.5\, a_{2m-1,1} \\
a_{2m,l} &= 0.5\left[(l - 2m - 2)a_{2m-1,l-1} - (l+1)a_{2m-1,l+1}\right] \\
a_{2m,2m+1} &= -1.5\, a_{2m-1,2m-2} \\
a_{2m,2m} &= -a_{2m-1,2m-1}
\end{aligned}
$$

For $2m$ is even, $2m - 1$ is odd. And for odd l, $l - 1$ is even. Use the induction hypothesis, all the odd index terms are zero.

The similar proof applied to odd order (n) polynomial. $\blacksquare$

Based on the above properties, we can now write $\Sigma_n(\omega)$ as

$$
\Sigma_n(\omega) = \frac{(-1)^n}{(n-1)!}\,\frac{g_{n-2}\left(\cos\frac{\omega}{2}\right)}{\sin^n\frac{\omega}{2}}. \tag{B.9}
$$

By combining (B.9) and (B.3), we obtain

$$
H_p(\omega) = \left(\cos\frac{\omega}{2}\right)^{2p+2}\sqrt{\frac{g_{4p+2}\left(\cos\frac{\omega}{2}\right)}{g_{4p+2}(\cos\omega)}},
$$

and

$$
|G_p(\omega)| = |H_p(\omega + \pi)| = \left(\sin\frac{\omega}{2}\right)^{2p+2}\sqrt{\frac{g_{4p+2}\left(\sin\frac{\omega}{2}\right)}{g_{4p+2}(\cos\omega)}}.
$$

From Eqs. (B.9), (B.1) and (B.2), we obtain,

$$
\Phi_p(\omega) = \left[\frac{\sin(\omega/2)}{(\omega/2)}\right]^{2p+2}\sqrt{\frac{(4p+3)!}{2^{4p+4}g_{4p+2}\left(\cos\frac{\omega}{2}\right)}},
$$

$$
\Psi_p(\omega) = e^{-j\frac{\omega}{2}}\left(\sin\frac{\omega}{4}\right)^{2p+2}\left[\frac{\sin(\omega/4)}{(\omega/4)}\right]^{2p+2}\sqrt{\frac{(4p+3)!\,g_{4p+2}\left(\sin\frac{\omega}{4}\right)}{2^{4p+4}g_{4p+2}\left(\cos\frac{\omega}{2}\right)g_{4p+2}\left(\cos\frac{\omega}{4}\right)}},
$$

and therefore,

$$
\Phi_p(0) = \sqrt{\frac{(4p+3)!}{2^{4p+4}g_{4p+2}(1)}}, \quad \Psi_p(0) = 0.
$$

Having derived analytical expressions, we shall be able to calculate these three functions of any order at any frequency point.

B.2   Numerical Computation Using FFT

The three functions that we investigated in the last section are continuous functions in the frequency domain. To compute their waveforms in the time domain, we used the FFT (Fast Fourier Transform) approach.

$H_p(\omega)$ is a 2π-periodic function. It is Discrete Fourier Transform of quadrature mirror filter $h(n)$ which is a discrete function in time domain. Recall that sampling in unit circle of frequency domain results in periodic extension of $h(n)$ in time domain. However, if the sampling period is small enough, aliasing in time domain is negligible and $h(n)$ obtained will be accurate. The sampling values of the $H_p(\omega)$ can be obtained:

$$H_p(k) = \left(\cos\frac{\pi k}{N}\right)^{2p+2} \sqrt{\frac{g_{4p+2}(\cos\frac{\pi}{N}k)}{g_{4p+2}(\cos\frac{2\pi}{N}k)}},\ 0 \le k \le N - 1.$$

Functions $\Phi(\omega)$ and $\Psi(\omega)$ are Fourier transforms of scaling function $\phi(t)$ and wavelet $\psi(t)$, respectively. Notice that functions $\phi(t)$ and $\psi(t)$ are continuous functions in time domain. By numerical method, we can only obtain sampling values in time domain. Recall that DFT (Discrete Fourier Transform) of sampling values $\phi(nT)$ and $\psi(nT)$ are related to the Fourier transform of continuous functions $\phi(t)$ and $\psi(t)$ by [49]:

$$\Phi_D(e^{j\omega}) = \frac{1}{T}\sum_{k=-\infty}^{\infty} \Phi(\frac{\omega}{T} - \frac{2\pi k}{T}),\ \ \Psi_D(e^{j\omega}) = \frac{1}{T}\sum_{k=-\infty}^{\infty} \Psi(\frac{\omega}{T} - \frac{2\pi k}{T}),$$

where T is the sampling period.

If the sampling frequency is high enough such that $f_s = \frac{1}{T} \gg f_h$, where f_h is the highest frequency component in $\phi(t)$ or $\psi(t)$, aliasing can be neglected. In this case, we can write:

$$\Phi_D(e^{j\omega}) = \frac{1}{T}\Phi(\frac{\omega}{T}),\ \ \Psi_D(e^{j\omega}) = \frac{1}{T}\Psi(\frac{\omega}{T}),\ \ -\pi \le \omega \le \pi.$$

Table B.1: Coefficients of $g_{24}(x)$ (a) and Truncated Impulse Response of $h_1(n)$ (b).

(a)			(b)	
k	$a_{24,k}$		n	$h_1(n)$
0	3679416778537.75		0	0.54173576
2	475582801692177.0		1	0.30682964
4	8011347151626016.5		2	-0.03549798
6	40907559988277171.5625		3	-0.07780792
8	81471913154443867.5		4	0.02268462
10	69736261315895408.25		5	0.02974682
12	26157606919852821.0		6	-0.01214549
14	4123375115615239.5		7	-0.01271542
16	243456149817686.25		8	0.00614143
18	4245937488920.0		9	0.00579932
20	13213718716.5		10	-0.00307863
22	2097148.875		11	-0.00274529
24	0.25		12	0.00154624

Note: $h_p(-n) = h_p(n)$

To use FFT to compute values $\phi(nT)$ and $\psi(nT)$, we need to sample functions $\Phi_D(e^{j\omega})$ and $\hat{\Psi}_D(e^{j\omega})$ as:

$$\Phi_D(k) = \begin{cases} \frac{1}{T}\Phi\left(\frac{2\pi k}{NT}\right) & ,0 \leq k \leq \frac{N}{2}, \\ \Phi_D(N-k) & ,\frac{N}{2} < k \leq (N-1). \end{cases}$$

and,

$$\Psi_D(k) = \begin{cases} \frac{1}{T}\Psi\left(\frac{2\pi k}{NT}\right) & ,0 \leq k \leq \frac{N}{2}, \\ \Psi_D(N-k) & ,\frac{N}{2} < k \leq (N-1). \end{cases}$$

Sampling values $\phi(nT)$ and $\psi(nT)$ can then be obtained from inverse FFT of the $\Phi_D(k)$ and $\Psi_D(k)$, respectively.

On the issue of implementation, we notice that coefficients of the polynomial $g_n(x)$ is growing very fast. As an example, the coefficients of $g_{24}(x)$ is shown in Table B.1. In our numerical calculations, 64-bit precision was used. Notice that $g_n(x)$ appears in both numerator and denominator of the formulae of $H_p(\omega)$. This suggests another way of preventing overflow in calculating $H_p(\omega)$ by using $k(n)g_n(x)$, where $k(n)$ is an appropriate multiplier and should be embedded into the iterative process of (B.6).

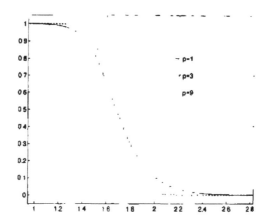

Figure B.1: Transition Band of Filters $H_p(\omega)$ with $p = 1, 3, 9$.

As the order p of the filter increases, the filter $H_p(\omega)$ is closer to the ideal halfband filter. Figure B.1 showed transition band of filters with $p = 1, 3, 9$.

Two MATLAB m-files for calculating QMF of the B-L wavelets are listed in the following.

```
function [H,G] = Lfilter(p,N)
% This function build a Quadrature Mirror Filter pair H, G
% H: low-pass filter; G: high-pass filter
% p: 2p + 1 is the order of Lemarie wavelet
% N : length of the filters
L = 4*p + 2;
C = gcoef(L);       % length of C is L+1
H = zeros(1, N);
G = zeros(1, N);
H(1) = sqrt(2);     % at w=0, H=√2
H(N/2 + 1) = 0.0;   % at w = π ,H=0
dw = 2 * pi/N;
for i = 1 : N/2 - 1
    omega = i * dw;
    u = 0;
    v = 0;
    for k = 1 : 2 : L + 1
        v = v + C(k) * cos(omega/2)^(k-1);
        u = u + C(k) * cos(omega)^(k-1);
    end;
    H(i + 1) = sqrt(2)*cos(omega/2)^(2*p + 2)*sqrt(v/u);
end;
H(N/2 + 2 : N) = H(N/2 : -1 : 2);
omega = [0 : N - 1] * dw;
G = -exp(-j * omega). * [H(N/2 + 1 : N), H(1 : N/2)];
```

```
function [c] = gcoef(n)
c = zeros(1, n+1);
t = zeros(1, n+1);
c(1) = 0.25;
c(2) = 0;
if( n > 8 )
    k = n/4;
else
    k = n;
end;
for i=1:1:n
    for j = 0 : 1 : i
        if j == 0
           t(1) = -0.5*c(2);
        elseif( j>0 & (j <= i-2) )
           t(j + 1) = 0.5 * ((j - i - 2)*c(j) - (j + 1)*c(j + 2));
        elseif j == (i - 1)
           t(j + 1) = -1.5*c(i - 1);
        else
           t(j + 1) = -c(i);
        end;
    end;
    if( i > k )    % apply multiplier
        c(1 : i + 1) = t(1 : i + 1)/(i - k);
    else
        c(1 : i + 1) = t(1 : i + 1);
    end;
end;
```

APPENDIX C
NUMERICAL COMPUTATION OF THE UNCERTAINTY FACTOR

Eq. (3.7) defines the uncertainty factor of a *lowpass filter* in the continuous frequency domain. In order to compute uncertainty factors of filters in a filter bank, two issues need to be resolved. First, the definition for a lowpass filter has to be extended to bandpass and highpass filters. Second, the formulas have to be modified for computation in discrete frequency domain.

The general definition of the variance σ_ω of the frequency distribution, including bandpass filters, adopted by Liu and Akansu [40] is:

$$\sigma_\omega^2 = \frac{1}{2\pi E} \int_{-\pi}^{\pi} (\omega - \overline{\omega})^2 |F(e^{j\omega})|^2 d\omega,$$

where

$$\overline{\omega} = \frac{1}{2\pi E} \int_{-\pi}^{\pi} \omega |F(e^{j\omega})|^2 d\omega.$$

The drawback of applying this definition to bandpass filters is that for real filters $|F(e^{j\omega})| = |F(e^{-j\omega})|$ and thus $\overline{\omega} = 0$ and is not the central frequency of the passband. Therefore, this is not a fair comparison between lowpass and bandpass filters. Moreover, the variance σ_ω will also depend on the location of the passband due to the factor $(\omega - \overline{\omega})^2 = \omega^2$, and thus is not fair even among bandpass filters.

To overcome this problem, we notice that the idea behind the variance σ_ω is the energy distribution within a complete *passband*. For bandpass filters, a single passband in the positive frequency side should be used. We thus adopted the following definition:

$$\sigma_\omega^2 = \frac{\int_{\omega_l}^{\omega_h} (\omega - \omega_c)^2 |F(e^{j\omega})|^2 d\omega}{\int_{\omega_l}^{\omega_h} |F(e^{j\omega})|^2 d\omega}, \tag{C.1}$$

103

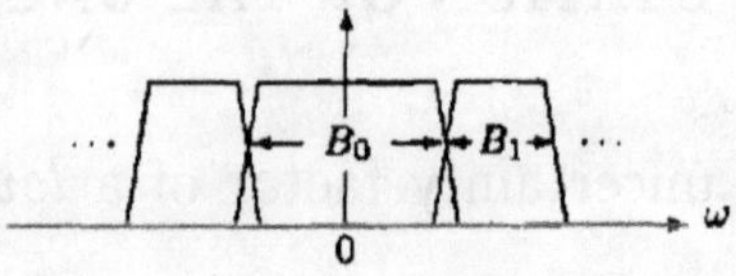

Figure C.1: Channel Bandwidths of Overcomplete Wavelet Representations.

$$\omega_c = \frac{\int_{\omega_l}^{\omega_h} \omega |F(e^{j\omega})|^2 d\omega}{\int_{\omega_l}^{\omega_h} |F(e^{j\omega})|^2 d\omega}, \tag{C.2}$$

where

$$\omega_l = \begin{cases} -\pi, \\ 0, \\ 0, \end{cases} \qquad \omega_h = \begin{cases} \pi, & \text{for lowpass filters,} \\ \pi, & \text{for bandpass filters,} \\ 2\pi, & \text{for highpass filters.} \end{cases}$$

Notice that this definition is good only for filters whose passband is completely contained in the range $[\omega_l, \omega_h]$, although sidebands are allowed within this range. Also notice that the bandwidth of the lowpass band is *twice* the width of bandpass bands by the construction of (3.3) as illustrated in Figure C.1.

In discrete frequency domain, Eqs. (C.1) and (C.2) should be modified as:

$$\sigma_\omega^2 = \frac{\sum_{k_l}^{k_h} (k - k_c)^2 |F(k)|^2}{\sum_{k_l}^{k_h} |F(k)|^2} \left(\frac{2\pi}{N}\right)^2,$$

$$k_c = \frac{\sum_{k_l}^{k_h} k |F(k)|^2}{\sum_{k_l}^{k_h} |F(k)|^2},$$

where N is the number of sampling points in the $[0, 2\pi]$, and

$$k_l = \begin{cases} -N/2, \\ 0, \\ 0, \end{cases} \qquad k_h = \begin{cases} N/2, & \text{for lowpass filters,} \\ N/2, & \text{for bandpass filters,} \\ N, & \text{for highpass filters.} \end{cases}$$

Notice that $|F(k)|$ is N-periodic such that $|F(k)| = |F(k + N)|$, and therefore $|F(-k)| = |F(N - k)|$.

Similarly, due to the periodic nature of the sequence $f(n)$ in the time domain, the variance σ_n should be modified as

$$\sigma_n^2 = \min_{0 < d < N} \frac{\sum_{n=0}^{N-1} (n - \overline{n})^2 |f(n + d)|^2}{\sum_{n=0}^{N-1} |f(n + d)|^2},$$

$$\overline{n} = \frac{\sum_{n=0}^{N-1} n |f(n + d)|^2}{\sum_{n=0}^{N-1} |f(n + d)|^2},$$

where $f(n+d)$ is the original $f(n)$ *circular* shifted by d.

A MATLAB function *ufactor()* for computing the uncertainty factor is included in the following. Also included is a MATLAB function *lwuf()* for building analyzing filters of an overcomplete wavelet packet using a prototype Lemarié filter and computing uncertainty factors of them, where the function $Lfilter()$ is given in Appendix B.

```
function [u]=ufactor(H)
% H is the Discrete Fourier Transform of a discrete filter h(n)
N = length(H);
W = H. * conj(H);
vmax = max(W);
if W(1) > 0.95*vmax          % low-pass filter
    F = [W(N/2 - 1 : N), W(1 : N/2)];
elseif W(N/2) > 0.95*vmax    % high-pass filter
    F = W;
else                         % band-pass filter
    F = W(1 : N/2);
end;
L = length(F);
fc = [0 : L-1] * F'/sum(F);
sf = (((0 : L-1] - fc). ∧ 2) * F'/sum(F)*(2*pi/N) ∧ 2;

% transform to time domain
h = real(ifft(H));
st = 1e10;
for d = 2 : N-1       % circular shift to find the minimum
    x = [h(d : N), h(1 : d-1)];
    W = x. ∧ 2;
    tc = [0 : N-1] * W'/sum(W);
    m = (((0 : N-1] - tc). ∧ 2) * W'/sum(W);
    if( m < st )
        st = m;
    end;
end;
u = st * sf;

function [] = lwuf(shell,p,nlevel)
% shell : =1, autocorrelation shell; =0, regular
% p : 2p + 1 is the order of Lemarie wavelet
% nlevel: number of levels
N = 2 ∧ nlevel;
SIZE = 256;
omega = 2*pi*[0 : SIZE-1]/SIZE;
[H, G] = Lfilter(p, SIZE);
H = H/sqrt(2);
G = G/sqrt(2);
if shell == 1
    H = H. * conj(H);
```

```
        G = G. * conj(G);
end;
W = ones(N, SIZE);
HH = ones(1, SIZE);
GG = ones(1, SIZE);
d = 1;
for n = 1 : nlevel
    HH = H(rem([0 : (SIZE−1)] * d, SIZE)+1);
    GG = G(rem([0 : (SIZE−1)] * d, SIZE)+1);
    for j = 2∧n : −2 : 1
        pt = ceil(j/2);
        if rem(pt, 2) = 0
            W(j, :) = W(pt, :). * GG;
            W(j−1, :) = W(pt, :). * HH;
        else
            W(j, :) = W(pt, :). * HH;
            W(j−1, :) = W(pt, :). * GG;
        end;
    end;
    d = d*2;
end;
clg;
mx = 1.1 * max(max(abs(W(:, :))));
for n = 1 : N
    f = abs(W(n, :));
    if n <= N/2
        plot(omega, f);
    else
        plot(omega, f,' :');
    end;
    uf = ufactor(W(n, :));
    str = sprintf('%.2f', uf);
    text(((n−1) + 0.1) * pi/N, 0.95*mx, str);
    if n==1
        axis([0 pi 0 mx]);
        hold;
    end;
end;
hold off;
of = sprintf('p%dl%ds%d.eps', p, nlevel, shell);
eval(['print -deps ' of]);
```

APPENDIX D
BOUNDARY TREATMENTS OF FINITE-LENGTH SEQUENCES

D.1   Periodic Extensions

For convolutions involving finite-length discrete sequences, we face the boundary problem. One solution is to construct an infinite-length signal from the finite-length sequence. For a finite-length sequence $s(n)$ of length N, two constructions are commonly used:

1) **N-Periodic extension.** An infinite-length signal $\tilde{s}(n)$ of period N is constructed as:

$$\tilde{s}(n) = \left\{ \begin{array}{ll} s(n) & , \ 0 \le n \le N-1 \\ s(n+N) & , \ -N \le n \le -1 \end{array} \right\} = \tilde{s}(n+kN).$$

This method is equivalent to a N-point FFT implementation of convolution. Since the periodic extension generally introduce discontinuities at boundaries, the output signal usually exhibits large artifacts near the boundaries.

2) **2N-Periodic mirror extension.** An infinite-length signal $\tilde{s}(n)$ of period $2N$ is constructed as:

$$\tilde{s}(n) = \left\{ \begin{array}{ll} s(n) & , \ 0 \le n \le N-1 \\ s(-n-1) & , \ -N \le n \le -1 \end{array} \right\} = \tilde{s}(n+2kN).$$

Since the new signal $\tilde{s}(n)$ is continuous at boundaries, the undesirable artifacts may be significantly reduced.

D.2   Closure of Symmetry Under Convolution

In order to define symmetric/antisymmetric sequences, we first define an expansion operator $\uparrow$ as:

$$\uparrow^m (s(n)) = \left\{ \begin{array}{ll} s(n/m) & , \ n = 0, \pm m, \pm 2m, \cdots, \\ 0 & , \ \text{otherwise.} \end{array} \right.$$

107

and denote $\uparrow^m (s(n))$ as $s_{\uparrow m}(n)$. Equivalently, we may write:

$$s_{\uparrow m}(n) = \sum_{k=-\infty}^{\infty} s(k)\delta(n - km).$$ (D.1)

We then define symmetric/antisymmetric sequences as:

Definition D.2.1 *For a discrete sequence $s(n)$, if there exist integers c and m such that $s_{\uparrow m}(c - n) = s_{\uparrow m}(c + n)$ $(s_{\uparrow m}(c - n) = -s_{\uparrow m}(c + n))$, the sequence is said to be symmetric (antisymmetric) at c/m, and $\mathcal{C} = c/m$ is said to be the symmetry center. For symmetry sequences, we may define a symmetry index $\mathcal{S}$: $\mathcal{S} = 1$ for symmetric sequences, and $\mathcal{S} = -1$ for antisymmetric sequences.*

Symmetry sequences possess some special properties. We will prove that symmetry sequences is closed under convolution. We first prove a proposition.

Proposition D.2.2 *The expansion operation is distributive over convolution:*

$$\uparrow^m (s * f)(n) = \uparrow^m (s(n)) * \uparrow^m (f(n)).$$

Proof: According to $(s * f)(n) = \sum_{k=-\infty}^{\infty} s(k)f(n - k)$ and (D.1), we have the left side:

$$
\begin{aligned}
\uparrow^m (s * f)(n) &= \sum_{l=-\infty}^{\infty} \sum_{k=-\infty}^{\infty} s(k)f(l - k)\delta(n - lm) \\
&= \sum_{k=-\infty}^{\infty} s(k) \sum_{l=-\infty}^{\infty} f(l - k)\delta(n - lm) \\
&= \sum_{k=-\infty}^{\infty} s(k) \sum_{i=-\infty}^{\infty} f(i)\delta(n - (i + k)m)
\end{aligned}
$$

and the right side:

$$
\begin{aligned}
\uparrow^m (s(n)) * \uparrow^m (f(n)) &= \sum_{k=-\infty}^{\infty} \sum_{l=-\infty}^{\infty} s(l)\delta(k - lm) \sum_{i=-\infty}^{\infty} f(i)\delta(n - k - im) \\
&= \sum_{l=-\infty}^{\infty} s(l) \sum_{i=-\infty}^{\infty} f(i) \sum_{k=-\infty}^{\infty} \delta(k - lm)\delta(n - k - im) \\
&= \sum_{l=-\infty}^{\infty} s(l) \sum_{i=-\infty}^{\infty} f(i)\delta(n - lm - im) \quad \blacksquare
\end{aligned}
$$

We now prove the closure property on convolution.

Theorem D.2.3 *Convolution of two symmetry sequences $s(n)$ and $f(n)$ results in a symmetry sequence $y(n)$ with symmetry index $S_y = S_x \cdot S_f$ and symmetry center $C_y = C_x + C_f$.*

Proof: Based on the given condition, we have:

$$x_{\uparrow m}(c_x - n) = S_x x_{\uparrow m}(c_x + n)$$
$$f_{\uparrow m}(c_f - n) = S_f f_{\uparrow m}(c_f + n)$$

Applying Proposition D.2.2, we have:

$$
\begin{aligned}
y_{\uparrow m}(c_x + c_f - n) &= \sum_{k=-\infty}^{\infty} x_{\uparrow m}(k) f_{\uparrow m}(c_x + c_f - n - k) \\
&= \sum_{l=-\infty}^{\infty} x_{\uparrow m}(c_x - l) f_{\uparrow m}(c_f - n + l) \\
&= \sum_{l=-\infty}^{\infty} S_x x_{\uparrow m}(c_x + l) S_f f_{\uparrow m}(c_f + n - l) \\
&= S_x S_f \sum_{k=-\infty}^{\infty} x_{\uparrow m}(k) f_{\uparrow m}(c_x + c_f + n - k) \\
&= S_x S_f y_{\uparrow m}(c_x + c_f + n) \quad \blacksquare
\end{aligned}
$$

Since translation of index n will not actually alter a discrete sequence, without loss of generality, symmetry sequences may be classified according to their symmetry index S and symmetry center C as below:

- **Type–I symmetric.** $s(n) = s(-n)$. The symmetry center $C = 0$.

- **Type–II symmetric.** $s(n) = s(-n-1)$. The symmetry center $C = -1/2$ ($c = -1, m = 2$). The $2N$-periodic mirror extended sequences introduced previously belong to this class.

- **Type–III symmetric.** $s(n) = s(-n+1)$. The symmetry center $C = 1/2$ ($c = 1, m = 2$).

- **Type–I antisymmetric.** $s(n) = -s(-n)$. The symmetry center $\mathcal{C} = 0$. Notice that $s(0) = 0$ is the constraint.

- **Type–II antisymmetric.** $s(n) = -s(-n-1)$. The symmetry center $\mathcal{C} = -1/2$ $(c = -1, m = 2)$.

- **Type–III antisymmetric.** $s(n) = -s(-n+1)$. The symmetry center $\mathcal{C} = 1/2$ $(c = 1, m = 2)$.

The closure property of symmetric sequences may reduce the computation burden significantly. For symmetric filters and mirror extension, we only need to carry out convolution on at most $N + 1$ sample points instead of $2N$.

REFERENCES

[1] Akram Aldroubi and Michael Unser, editors. *Wavelet in Medicine and Biology*. CRC Press, Boca Raton, Florida, 1996.

[2] H. C. Andrews and B. R. Hunt. *Digital Image Restoration*. Prentice Hall, Englewood Cliffs, New Jersey, 1989.

[3] M. R. Banham, N. P. Galatsanos, H. L. Gonzalez, and A. K. Katsaggelos. Multichannel restoration of single channel images using a wavelet-based subband decomposition. *IEEE Transactions on Image Processing*, 3:821–833, 1994.

[4] M. G. Bello. A combined Markov random field and wave-packet transform-based approach for image segmentation. *IEEE Transactions on Image Processing*, 3(6):834–846, 1994.

[5] Z. Berman and J. S. Baras. Properties of the multiscale maxima and zero-crossings representations. *IEEE Transactions on Signal Processing*, 41(12):3216–3231, 1993.

[6] A. C. Bovik. Analysis of multichannel narrowband filters for image texture segmentation. *IEEE Transaction on Signal Processing*, 39:2025–2043, 1991.

[7] P. Brodatz. *Textures-a Photographic Album for Artists and Designers*. Dover Publications, New York, 1966.

[8] T. Chang and C.-C J. Kuo. Texture analysis and classification with tree-structured wavelet transform. *IEEE Transaction on Image Processing*, 2(4):429–441, 1993.

[9] J. Chen and A. Kundu. Rotation and gray scale transform invariant texture identification using wavelet decomposition and hidden Markov model. *IEEE Transactions on Pattern Analysis and Machine Intelligence*, 16(2):208–214, 1993.

[10] R. R. Coifman and Y. Meyer. Orthonormal wavelet packet bases. preprint, Department of Mathematics, Yale University, 1990.

[11] I. Daubechies. Orthogonal bases of compactly supported wavelets. *Communications on Pure and Applied Mathematics*, XLI:909–996, 1988.

[12] I. Daubechies. The wavelet transform, time-frequency localization and signal analysis. *IEEE Transactions on Information Theory*, 36(5):961–1005, 1990.

[13] I. Daubechies. *Ten Lectures on Wavelets*. Society for Industrial and Applied Mathematics, Philadelphia, Pennsylvania, 1992.

[14] D. L. Donoho. Nonlinear solution of linear inverse problems by wavelet-vaguelette decomposition. Technical report, Department of Statistics, Stanford University, 1992.

[15] D. L. Donoho. Nonlinear wavelet methods for recovery of signals, densities, and spectra from indirect and noisy data. In *Proceedings of Symposia Applied Mathematics*, volume 00, pages 173–205, 1993.

[16] D. L. Donoho. Nonlinear solution of linear inverse problems by wavelet-vaguelette decomposition. *Applied and Computational Harmonic Analysis*, 2:101–126, 1995.

[17] D. L. Donoho and I. M. Johnstone. Ideal spatial adaptation via wavelet shrinkage. Technical report, Department of Statistics, Stanford University, 1992.

[18] R. O. Duda and P. E. Hart. *Pattern Classification and Scene Analysis*. John Wiley & Sons, New York, 1973.

[19] D. Dunn, W. E. Higgins, and J. Wakeley. Texture segmentation using 2-D Gabor elementary functions. *IEEE Transaction on Pattern Analysis Machine Intelligence*, 16(2):130-149, 1994.

[20] J. Fan and A. Laine. Multiscale contrast enhancement and denoising in digital radiographs. In Akram Aldroubi and Michael Unser, editors, *Wavelet in Medicine and Biology*, chapter 7, pages 163 189. CRC Press, 1996.

[21] D. Gabor. Theory of communication. *Journal of the IEE*, 93:429–457, 1946.

[22] R. C. Gonzalez and P. Wintz. *Digital Image Processing*. Addison-Wesley Publishing Company, Reading, Massachusetts, second edition, 1987.

[23] R. M. Haralick and L. G. Shapiro. Image segmentation techniques. *Comput. Vision Graphics Image Processing*, 29:100–132, 1985.

[24] J. Y. Hsiao and A. A. Sawchuk. Supervised textured image segmentation using feature smoothing and probabilistic relaxation techniques. *IEEE Transaction on Pattern Analysis Machine Intelligence*, 11:1279–1292, 1989.

[25] R. A. Hummel and S. W. Zucker. On the foundation of relaxation labeling processes. *IEEE Transactions on Pattern Analysis and Machine Intelligence*, 5(3):267–287, 1983.

[26] L. W. Couch II. *Digital and Analog Communication Systems*. Macmillan Publishing Company, New York, third edition, 1990.

[27] M. Kardan J. M. H. D. Buf and M. Span. Texture feature performance for image segmentation. *Pattern Recognition*, 23:291–309, 1990.

[28] A. K. Jain. *Fundamentals of Digital Image Processing*. Prentice Hall, Englewood Cliffs, New Jersey, 1989.

[29] A. K. Jain and R. C. Dubes. *Algorithms for Clustering Data*. Prentice Hall, Englewood Cliffs, New Jersey, 1988.

[30] A. K. Jain and F. Farrokhnia. Unsupervised texture segmentation using Gabor filters. *Pattern Recognition*, 24(12):1167–1186, 1991.

[31] B. Jawerth, M. L. Hilton, and T. L. Huntsberger. Local enhancement of compressed images. *Journal of Mathematical Imaging and Vision*, 3:39–49, 1993.

[32] B. Jawerth and W. Sweldens. An overview of wavelet based multiresolution analysis. *SIAM Review*, 36(3):377–412, 1994.

[33] A. K. Katsaggelos, editor. *Digital Image Restoration*. Springer-Verlag, New York, 1991.

[34] A. Kundu and J. Chen. Texture classification using QMF bank-based subband decomposition. *CVGIP: Graphical Models and Image Processing*, 54(5):369–384, 1992.

[35] A. Laine and J. Fan. An adaptive approach for texture segmentation by multi-channel wavelet frames. In *SPIE Proceedings on Mathematical Imaging: Wavelet Applications in Signal and Image Processing*, volume 2034, pages 288–299, 1993.

[36] A. Laine and J. Fan. Texture classification by wavelet packet signatures. *IEEE Transaction on Pattern Analysis Machine Intelligence*, 15(11):1186–1191, 1993.

[37] A. Laine and J. Fan. Frame representations for texture segmentation. *IEEE Transaction on Image Processing*, 5(5):771–780, 1996.

[38] A. Laine, S. Schuler, J. Fan, and W. Huda. Mammographic feature enhancement by multiscale analysis. *IEEE Transaction on Medical Imaging*, 13(4):725–740, 1994.

[39] A. Laine, S. Schuler, and V. Girish. Orthonormal wavelet representations for recognizing complex annotations. *Machine Vision and Applications*, 6:110–123, 1993.

[40] Y. Liu and A. N. Akansu. An evaluation of time-frequency localization in transforms and filter banks. In *IEEE International Conference on Acoustics, Speech and Signal Processing*, pages 261–263, 1993.

[41] S. Mallat. Multifrequency channel decompositions of images and wavelet methods. *IEEE Transaction on Acoustics, Speech and Signal Processing*, 37:2091–2110, 1989.

[42] S. Mallat. A theory for multiresolution signal decomposition: The wavelet representation. *IEEE Transactions on Pattern Analysis and Machine Intelligence*, 11:674–693, 1989.

[43] S. Mallat and W. L. Hwang. Singularity detection and processing with wavelets. *IEEE Transactions on Information Theory*, 38(2):617–643, 1992.

[44] S. Mallat and S. Zhong. Characterization of signals from multiscale edges. *IEEE Transactions on Pattern Analysis and Machine Intelligence*, 14(7):710–732, 1992.

[45] U. Manber. *Introduction to Algorithms - A Creative Approach*. Addision-Wesley Publishing Company, Reading, Massachusetts, 1989.

[46] P. Maragos, J. F. Kaiser, and T. F. Quatieri. On amplitude and frequency demodulation using energy operators. *IEEE Transactions on Signal Processing*, 41(4):1532–1550, 1993.

[47] D. Marr. *Vision*. W.H. Freeman and Company, New York, 1982.

[48] Pierre Moulin. Wavelet thresholding techniques for power spectrum estimation. *IEEE Transactions on Signal Processing*, 42(11):3126–3136, 1994.

[49] A. V. Oppenheim and R. W. Schafer. *Discrete-time Signal Processing*. Prentice Hall, Englewood Cliffs, New Jersey, 1989.

[50] B. Macq P. Desarte and D. T. Slock. Signal-adapted multiresolution transform for image coding. *IEEE Transactions on Information Theory*, 38(2):897–904, 1992.

[51] A. Papoulis. *Signal Analysis*. McGraw-Hill Book Company, New York, 1977.

[52] J.-C. Pesquet, H. Krim, and H. Carfantan. Time-invariant orthonormal wavelet representations. *IEEE Transaction on Signal Processing*, 44:1964–1970, 1996.

[53] L. R. Rabiner and R. W. Schafer. *Digital Processing of Speech Signals*. Prentice Hall, Englewood Cliffs, New Jersey, 1978.

[54] T. R. Reed and H. Wechesler. Segmentation of textured images and Gestalt organization using spatial/spatial-frequency representations. *IEEE Transaction on Pattern Analysis Machine Intelligence*, 12:1–12, 1990.

[55] K. H. Rosen. *Discrete Mathematics and Its Applications*. Random House, New York, 1988.

[56] S. A. Ruzinsky and E. T. Olsen. L_1 and L_∞ minimization via a variant of Karmarkar's algorithm. *IEEE Transaction on Acoustics, Speech, and Signal Processing*, 37:245–253, 1989.

[57] N. Saito. *Local Feature Extraction and Its Applications Using a Library of Bases*. PhD thesis, Yale University, 1994.

[58] E. P. Simoncelli, W. T. Freeman, E. H. Adelson, and D. J. Heeger. Shiftable multiscale transforms. *IEEE Transaction on Information Theory*, 38(2):587–607, 1992.

[59] G. Strang. Wavelets and dilation equations: a brief introduction. *SIAM Review*, 31(4):614–627, 1989.

[60] A. N. Tikhonov and V. Y. Arsenin. *Solution of Ill-posed Problems*. V. H. Winston & Sons, Washington, D. C., 1977.

[61] M. Tuceryan and A. K. Jain. Texture analysis. In C. H. Chen, L. F. Pau, and P. S. P. Wang, editors, *The Handbook of Pattern Recognition and Computer Vision*, pages 235–276. World Scientific Publishing Company, Singapore, 1993.

[62] M. Unser. Texture classification and segmentation using wavelet frames. *IEEE Transactions on Image Processing*, 4(11):1549–1560, 1995.

[63] P. P. Vaidyanathan. *Multirate Systems and Filter Banks*. Prentice-Hall, Englewood Cliffs, New Jersey, 1993.

[64] R. Wilson and M. Spann. Finite prolate spheroidal sequences and their applications II: image feature description and segmentation. *IEEE Transaction on Pattern Analysis Machine Intelligence*, 10:193–203, 1988.

BIOGRAPHICAL SKETCH

Jian Fan was born in Fuzhou City, Fujian Province, the People's Republic of China, on April 15, 1954. In 1978, he began his studies at the Xiamen University, Xiamen, PRC, where he received BS degree in radio physics (82) and MS degree in marine physics (85). From 1985 to 1989, he served in the faculty of the Oceanography Department of the Xiamen University. He arrived in the United States on January 13, 1989 to pursue graduate studies. He continued his studies at the University of Florida, Gainesville, where he received MS degrees in electrical engineering (90) and in computer and information sciences (92). He jointed the Hewlett-Packard Company as a software design engineer in 1995.

I certify that I have read this study and that in my opinion it conforms to acceptable standards of scholarly presentation and is fully adequate, in scope and quality, as a dissertation for the degree of Doctor of Philosophy.

Andrew F. Laine, Chairman
Associate Professor of Computer and
Information Science and Engineering

I certify that I have read this study and that in my opinion it conforms to acceptable standards of scholarly presentation and is fully adequate, in scope and quality, as a dissertation for the degree of Doctor of Philosophy.

Gerhard Ritter
Professor of Computer and
Information Science and Engineering

I certify that I have read this study and that in my opinion it conforms to acceptable standards of scholarly presentation and is fully adequate, in scope and quality, as a dissertation for the degree of Doctor of Philosophy.

Sartaj Sahni
Professor of Computer and
Information Science and Engineering

I certify that I have read this study and that in my opinion it conforms to acceptable standards of scholarly presentation and is fully adequate, in scope and quality, as a dissertation for the degree of Doctor of Philosophy.

Dave Wilson
Professor of Mathematics

I certify that I have read this study and that in my opinion it conforms to acceptable standards of scholarly presentation and is fully adequate, in scope and quality, as a dissertation for the degree of Doctor of Philosophy.

John G. Harris
Professor of Electrical and Computer
Engineering

This dissertation was submitted to the Graduate Faculty of the College of Engineering and to the Graduate School and was accepted as partial fulfillment of the requirements for the degree of Doctor of Philosophy.

August 1997

Winfred M. Phillips
Dean, College of Engineering

Karen A. Holbrook
Dean, Graduate School